This book is for you if:

- You are in a good relationship and don't want it to turn into the stereotypical, long-term, dull partnership...or worse!

- You are single and you want to find love that will enhance the fun in your life, not diminish your freedom.

- You see so many couples around you who aren't having fun and you don't want to end up like them.

- You want to understand why so many couples start with every intention of 'happily ever after' yet, for most, fun and laughter disappears after the seven-year itch.

- You hate partnerships in which just one wears the trousers rather than both choosing to wear shorts.

- You want your children to grow up in a home that teaches self-confidence, kindness and love, not toleration of incompatibility and censorship.

What people are saying about
The Coupledom Trap

"I would encourage anyone who is about to commit to a long term relationship to read this book with an open mind and a sense of humour...it might prevent a lot of heartache later!"

Sally Woods, Bachelor of Arts (Hons) in Integrative-Relational Counselling

"Do not pass this book without reading it; whichever stage of a relationship you are in, this book will improve the way you live your life. For me, *The Coupledom Trap* is the most honest and direct approach to how we should be looking at our relationships. It not only explains the problem, but Tal Araim seems to have found the cure.

Quite simply, this book is the penicillin for our generation and, most importantly, the next."

Simon Clark, Former Publishing Director, Dennis Publishing UK Men's Lifestyle and Maxim Magazine

"Anyone who is exploring relationships or planning to commit long-term will benefit from reading this book."

Jacqui Hughes, UKCP registered psychotherapist and supervisor

About Tal Araim, author of *The Coupledom Trap*

Tal Araim was born in Baghdad, Iraq in 1966. His family moved to London in 1980 where he still lives.

In 1988, he graduated from Imperial College with a degree in Computing Science and pursued a career in catering, eventually running his own Hawaiian restaurant for 20 years.

This experience led to his interest in observing people's interactions with each other and to study human behaviour and psychology. His scientific background gave him the tools to analyse and formulate the data that he collected.

After 30 years, which included many relationships, a marriage, two children, an affair, a near divorce, clinical depression, drugs, alcohol, therapy, recovery, and research, Tal channelled his experiences and knowledge into giving seminars, taking part in countless debates and, finally, in writing this book.

Acknowledgements

This book is a lifelong project that started on that day in 1977 when I asked a certain girl whether she wanted to move down three rows and sit next to me in the social club cinema. My research began that very moment. Therefore, I have to thank her as well as every other person with whom I have shared an emotional experience.

As for the actual act of writing this book, there are many friends and colleagues who were extremely selfless with their input. To each and every one, I am eternally grateful. There are some whom I would like to give special mention.

I would like to thank Maggie Chapman, co-founder of City Minds, for her invaluable feedback. I am also eternally grateful to Sue Marchant, my editor, who transformed this book from sounding like a drunken rant on a bar stool to its intended purpose of helping build more fulfilling relationships. A special mention goes to my brother, Oday. First, as a qualified relationship counsellor and member of the British Association for Counselling & Psychotherapy, he helped me turn many of my personal observations into universally applicable and sound advice that readers can relate to regardless of their personal stories. Second, because he is my brother, he flagged any hint of denial or delusion in which I may have found reason to indulge. And third...

Even though most of the references in this book use the examples of heterosexual relationships, all of the theories and analyses apply to any type of relationship.

The Coupledom Trap is my gift to my daughters so that, hopefully, they will one day live in a world that discourages lovelessness and encourages honesty and love.

A Gift for you...

After reading this book, go onto **www.compass4couples.com** home page and do the Compatibility Test. You will receive a report on your relationship as it is today. The aim is to find out what you both really think about each other and your relationship.

We all want to increase the fun and honesty in our home life. Let this test be a step towards this end.

Remember, do it once you have finished reading the book.

I hope you enjoy...

"WHY IS THE WORLD FULL OF COUPLES WITH LONELY HEARTS?"

THE COUPLEDOM TRAP

Have the COURAGE to be HONEST and
GUIDE YOURSELF AWAY from the
stereotypical TRAP and into HAPPINESS

TAL ARAIM

Published by Filament Publishing Ltd

16 Croydon Road, Beddington, Croydon,

Surrey, CRO 4PA, United Kingdom.

+44(0)20 8688 2598

www.filamentpublishing.com

The Coupledom Trap by Tal Araim

ISBN 978-1-911425-53-3

Illustrations by Ed Merricks

Contents

1

WHY AM I WRITING THIS?

I was married on the ninth day of the ninth month in the year nineteen ninety-nine.

It was a familiar story — we fell in love. Optimism was high, and the world was a wonderful place. We experienced the usual excitement intermingled with trepidation and finally took the plunge.

Within a year, cracks started appearing in the idyllic picture. Nevertheless, we persevered and attributed our diminishing passion to the introduction of life's realities. Some time passed before we decided to have children, which I hoped would somehow bring back the "magic." We had two daughters who instantly  became our life and joy. For a while, the children brought us closer together, but the constant task of friction avoidance eventually replaced the effortless, playful intimacy of yesteryear. We got on with our lives because that was what we were supposed to do to maintain the status quo.

Then I found love or, rather, love found me. I did not go out and actively look for new love. She appeared from within my circle of friends. I immediately felt that this love was different: the kind you only read about — the kind that allowed me to accept and love myself because another person accepted my faults and frailties. This love lasted for two years, until I reached the inevitable moment when either the marriage or the affair had to end.

Many factors came into play, not least how unfair it was to my wife, but my number one consideration was the effect of any decision on my relationship with my daughters. The thought of risking our relationship was too unbearable to even contemplate. Rightly or wrongly, we ended the affair and have not seen each other since.

Of course, I went through the inevitable period of grieving about the loss of a love, but I eventually decided to try to find out why this happened. Surely, I was not just the typical man going through the typical midlife crisis cliché.

There is something else that makes us susceptible to straying. Even though I was not available on the outside, my heart obviously was on the inside. I soon discovered that I was not alone. There is an epidemic going around that no one dares to acknowledge. The world is too full of couples who do not love each other but "just get on with it," couples who are committed on the outside but not on the inside. Most of us play the part of a committed partner, but our hearts do not share in this commitment. We fool ourselves by saying that this coexistence is good enough: better the devil you know, the grass is not always greener...and so on.

We easily pass judgement and say that those who divorce or separate just do not have the stamina needed to make a marriage work. After closer observation, however, I could not help but see that those who tolerate loveless relationships do so because they are comfortable enough to do so. They fill their cups of happiness elsewhere — with friends, lovers, children, extended family, hobbies, jobs, good health, money, or status. It is when some of these sources of comfort disappear that people reassess and make life-changing decisions. I was convinced that this was the elephant in the room.

Such avoidance of "the elephant" perhaps caused me to glorify the new love I had found. After all, I had not lived with this other woman. I had not paid a gas bill or fought about the in-laws with her. Even if my love for her felt real, it was not truly tested. I could not, hand on heart, say that if I ended up living with her, we would have had a wonderful life.

However, I also cannot deny the fact that my heart was available. The reason for this availability is our ubiquitous toleration of lovelessness in the name of the realities of life. What I wanted to know was what damage this toleration of lovelessness was doing to us and, more importantly, to our children. And even if we conclude that we are unwittingly causing damage to our children, what can we do about it?

I began to engage in a number of searching conversations with many of my friends and colleagues, those with children in particular, and subsequently with several random volunteers.

It was becoming more and more apparent that my situation was not only common, but it was also representative of the overwhelming majority. It seems we find it acceptable to continue living with partners whom we no longer love or who no longer love us.

We explain and justify the situation by claiming that this is just the way it is. Love cannot last when life takes over. We do not even acknowledge it — quite the opposite. We perfect the art of pretending to be in love, the art of believing in our *comfortable illusion of love*. We buy the presents, receive the Valentine's Day cards, call each other "honey" and "sweetheart," and put on happy faces in public. But we do it out of habit or duty. The minute we are alone with our partners, our smiles tend to fade. We revert back to playing more insular roles. Inner thoughts are withheld or, at least, carefully phrased. We interact with care and attention in order to avoid friction and to maintain our comfortable illusions. This applies to all of our interactions ranging from our sexual satisfaction, to how we really feel about going out with Mike and Sandra next weekend.

With the advent of modern communication, it's not uncommon to find ourselves physically in the presence of our partners but mentally elsewhere, engaging in cybertalk. We often call our friends when our partners are not around so that we can talk freely. We play the politics of cohabitation to minimise pain, not to maximise pleasure. We justify our acceptance of this behaviour because so many around us do the exact same thing. Slowly but surely, our relationships change from pleasure to management.

What is even harder to understand is how we encourage others to practice lovelessness without realising it. Think about it. When a friend tells us that he or she has decided to get married, even though we may have a strong suspicion that our friend is not in love with the partner-to-be, or vice versa, we nevertheless wish both of them the best. We even join in the excitement of planning the bachelor or bachelorette party and the wedding itself and ignore our duty to ask the important questions: "Do you two have a strong and true enough love that will make the realities of life pleasurable, or will life get the better of you and, in time, leave you loveless?" We do not ask these questions, and lovelessness increases while we watch.

I wanted to know whether I was just being overemotional because of my own experiences or whether the statistics supported my belief that there was a problem and we needed to do something about it.

In the United States, 57 per cent of marriages end in divorce. The rate is slightly lower in the United Kingdom and other European countries.[1] The statement "one in two marriages fail" has become an acceptable cliché. Most of the couples that stay together do so because of fear of the unknown, financial obligations, children, or some other form of social or self-imposed sense of commitment.

According to a survey carried out on a cross section of American couples, 83 per cent said they knew they did not have love in their relationships but they "just got on with it."[2] It is also estimated that by the end of 2016, the number of parents in the United Kingdom who will have children out of wedlock will be higher than those who are married.[3] This is becoming common in many Western societies. The popularity of marriage is declining, but the number of family breakdowns is not.

The annual UK budget for dealing with family breakdown was at an all-time high of £24 billion ($40 billion) in 2011.[4] By 2014, it had risen to £46 billion ($75 billion). That equates to £1,500 ($2,500) per taxpayer.[5] Why is this acceptable? Such statistics in other areas of life would not be so casually tolerated. Can you imagine if one in every two car trips ended up in an accident? Would we let our children drive? More scrutiny is applied to obtaining a pet licence than to a marriage licence. Why do we accept this lottery in the name of romance?

I wanted to see how we got to this state of accepting lovelessness. Why do we undervalue the positive influence of love? If you have ever been in love, real love in which the ecstatic feeling of day one becomes even stronger by day one thousand, you would know exactly how you effortlessly become a source of optimism and forgiveness of human fallibility. You begin to overflow with goodwill.

We should live with someone we truly love. I do not mean someone with whom we can comfortably coexist; I mean someone whose presence makes us feel alive, childlike, daring, unique, and proud to be exactly who we truly are. Being with such a partner brings out our best qualities. It maximises our potential good and greatly helps us on our journey of self-awareness. Aren't we selling ourselves short by not demanding that we have such love in our lives? We are far better creatures when we are in love. We are shadows of our true selves when we live in loveless partnerships.

We are expected to have the foresight of Nostradamus when we choose our long-term partners. No matter how certain we are that we have found "the one," we have to leave room for a possible change of heart and mind. We need a new outlook on relationships that allows us to gradually find out and accept who we are so that we become better equipped to know what and who we want. Continual honest assessment is missing from our relationship framework. Instead, we applaud withholding inner thoughts and feelings in the name of mature compromise. The result is underachievement in our relationships, in our parenting, and in our overall happiness. We need to live better.

I wrote *The Coupledom Trap* in the hope that my daughters will one day live in a world where true love is abundant.

2

THE STORY OF COUPLEDOM

Let us take a trip back to our cave days.

At some point in our evolutionary history, we decided that this solo roaming-around thing wasn't going well for us. That was when man became a social animal in the hope of improving chances of survival.

Men and women started living in groups of 30 or so. The children belonged to the group, and anyone could have sex with anyone else.

Two types of relationships gradually emerged. The first developed when we realised that pairing up with another human being could complement our strengths and increase the likelihood of achieving the common goals necessary for survival such as hunting, fetching water, gathering food, and protecting the group.

Men and women worked together and, at some point, inevitably would become aware of their co-worker's irritating traits. Was it at this point that we learned to tolerate for the greater good? If my fellow caveman hunter displayed annoying habits, I would probably have chosen to ignore them because we had a common goal of survival. Therefore, our toleration level very much depends on the beneficial return we are receiving from a relationship.

Let us call this relationship a DO relationship, in which we continue to tolerate each other as long as we are doing what we're supposed to be doing to achieve our common survival goals. We focus on the good points and learn to tolerate the bad, and as long as the benefits keep coming, the relationship continues.

So how do we find a DO companion? We look for someone who has the strengths that, when combined with our strengths, will help us achieve our common functional goals. We exhibit alertness during the recruitment process and, once our DO companion is found, we identify our respective roles and focus our attention on the common goal we aim to achieve. Adrenaline flows as we execute our respective chores within this mutually beneficial relationship. Therefore, *we show off our strengths* when looking for a DO companion.

The other type of relationship that evolved was for an entirely different purpose and probably started around the campfire.

At the end of a hard day, we would gather around the warmth of the flames to rest and reflect. Perhaps one person noticed something fanciful: a shooting star, an insect, and reacted by smiling, snorting, and giggling with pleasure. Maybe just one other person around that campfire was able to identify with the feeling and started to smile, snort, and giggle with pleasure, too. These two then spent the rest of the evening pointing, snorting, and giggling together.

This relationship had no functional goal or benefit at all. Hitting it off like that was not dependent on either person's ability to hunt or fight or gather or cook. However, it increased the level of serotonin secreted in the two gigglers' brains. Serotonin is a neurotransmitter that enables us to experience pleasure. This secretion produced a pleasurable, relaxed feeling that countered the alertness of the adrenalin secreted earlier that day.

Let us call this a BE relationship in which we continue to like the other person because they are being themselves: being silly, or truthful, or expressing some pleasurable inner emotion which, in turn, brings us pleasure.

The recruiting process for such a BE companion is therefore different from that of a DO companion. If there were a *How to Find a BE Companion* guide, it would advise us to reveal our silly sides, our mischief, and our thoughts, and to demonstrate the actions that bring us pleasure, that make us relax, that make us snort and giggle. We need to allow our brains to roam freely so that they can find the next giggling source.

To be able to let our brains roam with such freedom, we need to accept that there will be moments when we unwittingly reveal another flaw in ourselves or we stumble across a flaw in our partners. Embrace these moments, for they are the very moments that will determine whether we are compatible — whether we are BE companions.

It is endearing when friends can comfortably point out each other's flaws without censorship: "You're short." "You're fat." "Your nose is crooked." "You talk too much." What such expressions are really saying is this: "I am aware of your flaws, and I like you anyway." If such exchanges lead to moments of joint pleasure, then we may have found our BE companion. We continue to reveal our flaws and silliness and see whether this continues to bring us pleasure. Therefore, *we need to reveal our flaws* to recruit a BE companion.

Our functional strengths play no part in the recruitment of a BE companion. Even if they are mentioned, it is purely for the purpose of sharing information. As long as we have mutual pleasure, our BE companionships will continue to grow. Today, we might hear someone say, "Jane knows everything about me. I trust her with my life. We always have such a laugh together, and I really can tell her anything." In a Darwinian sense, this must have evolved from that campfire experience. Jane is a fellow snorting giggler.

All human relationships fall somewhere between DO and BE. Some have more DO, and some have more BE. DO relationships have higher levels for tolerating incompatible traits because there is a common, survival-based, functional goal that bonds two people together and helps them justify toleration of their incompatibilities. If you take away that goal, the toleration level declines severely.

Back to the story of coupledom:

When we lived in groups, the alpha males got their unfair share of the spoils in every sense. At some point, the beta males must have become tired of getting little in the way of sexual favours or, indeed, of sharing survival-based goals with a woman and decided that enough was enough.[6]

Eventually, a pioneering beta male may have found a female willing to listen, perhaps because she was not favoured by the alpha males, and asked whether she was happy being a secondary priority. This beta man then "proposed" the scenario of returning every day to her, to protect her, to hunt for food for her, and to protect their future children until they could fend for themselves. In return, she intimated a willingness to protect their cave while he was away, cook, have sex with him, and give birth to their children.

In all probability, her reasoning would have been: "So are you like a really great hunter and a strong guy and stuff? Well, if you are, this actually makes sense. I'm sick of grovelling around the alpha males. I want food, and I want protection for my children and myself. Why not? Let's give it a go." And thus began coupling — a partnership with a mutually beneficial, functional goal. This coupling belongs very much in the DO domain.

From the moment of the beta males' social revolution until about 150 years ago, coupling openly belonged in the world of DO.[7] Throughout the ages, whether it was executing chores, protecting possessions, or ensuring offspring legitimacy, tasks were divided according to gender. Men and women got together for common functional goals that had nothing to do with fulfilling the snorting and giggling needs of the individuals. We recruited partners using DO adrenalin-inducing techniques. We had to meet our serotonin needs elsewhere.

One person may tell the other, "You're great. I'm thrilled you're my partner. But now I'm going out to chill, point at stars, and giggle in a silly, relaxed way with someone else." The other partner might understand that their union is not about snorting and giggling. Therefore, that person, too, can go outside the relationship to satisfy giggling needs.

Now, things have changed. A partner can no longer tell the other, "I think you are wonderful in the way you carry out your part of our functional needs so well, but on weekends, I prefer to go out with friends who are silly and funny. I will do this because I need to laugh and relax after a long, hard week and, let's face it, you are not really my go-to person for fun, laughter, mental relaxation, or pleasure."

Nowadays, no one would accept this proposition. Nor should they. We want to be each other's campfire gigglers, and this is a wonderful thing. It means we've abolished gender roles. We do not partner up to divide chores. We partner up because we love each other irrespective of how well we cook or mow or earn.

25

These have become secondary issues. Finally, the sexes are truly equal. We want each other primarily to fulfil our emotional needs.

We have decided that we want our chosen partner to be our mental-pleasure partner, our snorting giggler. A partnership now is very much a BE relationship. How warm one makes the other feel inside is far more important than how well that person executes functional tasks.

But there is a problem. When we are looking for a partner, even though we claim we want a BE companion, we still recruit using DO techniques. We still show off our functional strong points, and we hide our silliness and flaws. We apologise for, understate, or even hide our childish, pleasurable, silly indulgences. We instinctively prefer to hide the simplest and most innocent of our flaws that bring us giggles. Hiding flaws is a great technique if you're at a job interview, but this is a calamitous technique if you're searching for a BE companion.

Hiding our indulgent silliness is damaging our chances of finding out the truth about our giggling compatibilities. At the start of a relationship, we hide and edit and censor and impress for a considerable amount of time. We may find it difficult to acknowledge later that we are not gigglers together and, instead of ending the relationship, we use our hardwired DO toleration skills to keep it going.

However, our DO toleration skills work only if there is a common survival goal acting as a bond. The strength of this bond very much depends on how much the partners need each other to achieve their common functional goals. In liberal societies, we can do anything without a partner and not be shunned. A single man or woman can get any job, take part in any activity, and even become a parent or adopt a child. Few will begrudge such lifestyle choices. Family and friends generally accept such situations. A man or a woman no longer *needs* to be in a partnership to get a mortgage or a membership in a social club, or have a child registered for the local school, or follow a certain religion.

Even if we think there is a functional need to be together, for example, if one partner is the breadwinner and the other chooses to tolerate, this is a personal decision and a lifestyle choice — not a society-imposed necessity. If the tolerating partner wishes to leave the partnership and earn, society will embrace this decision. If parents decide that it is better for their children to stop hearing them bicker as a couple and start seeing them as friends who don't live together, society will not stand in their way. Therefore, there is no functional goal left to tie two non-gigglers together, and the increases in divorce and separation seem to corroborate this.

We need to realise that the only way a partnership can be pleasurable in the long term is if it is a BE companionship. We no longer want or need our partnerships to be DO based. To find such a BE companionship, we must recruit using BE, not DO, techniques. This takes us to the heart of the issue: we still recruit our partners using DO techniques. We hide our perceived flaws and giggling pursuits when we meet someone we like. Before we know it, a DO relationship becomes the status quo.

Let us say that I love to sing in public now and then because it brings me pleasure. I happen to be out on a date. The conversation flows naturally, the topics are varied, and the evening is going well. However, we then move on to talk about behaviour that we find embarrassing, and she acknowledges how much she cringes at the thought of anyone singing along in a karaoke bar. She then says, "Please don't tell me you're one of them." Decision moment. What should I reveal: the absolute truth or some edited version of it?

I decide on the latter option, and the relationship continues. On the whole, I genuinely enjoy my time with her and can see many positives. I may therefore forgo my karaoke excursions because they have become part of my "single past." I tell myself that I've moved on. I'm now part of a committed, serious relationship with the inevitable compromises. Surely, losing the karaoke nights is a small price to pay to prolong this partnership. I therefore justify denying myself this pleasure.

On the other hand, I could continue to enjoy the occasional karaoke night out but not tell her about it. I justify this decision by saying that it happens once every couple of months; therefore, why annoy her by telling her? It's such an insignificant part of our relationship.

Sometimes we don't conceal a pleasure; we simply limit it. I may choose to reveal my soft spot for the odd karaoke night, but I belittle it and agree with her that it is a silly indulgence. So when my friends ask me to go, I may reply, "Let me see if I've earned enough brownie points first." She may have made other plans for us that night, but even if she hasn't, she may be upset that I would rather hang around with my silly friends who do nothing but get drunk and sing. Perhaps she comments on my immaturity, so I avoid the whole subject because I genuinely care for her. I end up waiting for her to plan a night out with her friends and then see whether my silly, singing friends want to go to a karaoke bar.

This is acceptable logic, and it applies to many aspects of relationship communication. Pleasure becomes a currency.

When it comes to relationships, we have brainwashed ourselves into believing that compromise means editing or withholding certain thoughts, when in fact the very opposite is true. **The only way to achieve** genuine compromise in a relationship is by revealing the full truth and seeing how each partner can accommodate the other's needs and pleasures based on full disclosure. We need to allow our brains to relax and fully reveal their uncensored, unique selves. Our partners can then decide if they find them beautiful and liberating or something they can neither comprehend nor admire.

Is it OK to like only some parts of the mind but not the rest? The parts we like must be enough to make the parts we don't like pleasurably tolerable. Toleration needs to be minimal to maintain the shared giggling pleasures. The smiles and intimate warm feeling must still exist. Otherwise, we would need a functional goal we can achieve only by coupling to keep the partnership going. Therein lies the problem. We no longer need each other for such functional needs.

Our newly-found freedoms for the individual and the abolishment of gender-defined roles are wonderful achievements that we need to celebrate and embrace. However, we must change our love partner interview techniques from the ones we use to find DO companions to those we use to find BE companions. These techniques are currently reserved for finding close friends. We need to reveal the flaws, the differences, and the mischief. If I like singing and hate rugby and she loves rugby but hates singing, then we need to reveal our likes and dislikes to each other from day one to determine whether we can incorporate both activities into our lives.

Going back to my first date, the minute she told me that she hated karaoke, I should have grabbed her by the hand and taken her to the nearest karaoke bar to sing my heart out. If she then said, "I think it's time to call it a night," and decided that she did not want to pursue the relationship, then we could have saved our future children a lifetime of witnessing their parents bicker. If, on the other hand, she said, "I still hate singing, but I love that smile on your face when you sing," then we may have been onto something.

She must love to see me have fun, and I must equally, effortlessly, and genuinely love to see her enjoying her rugby games. If I watch rugby with her and make her feel that I am doing it under duress, then I am being selfish. I am, in effect, saying, "What's in it for me?" Such a relationship is as DO as it gets.

Going our separate ways to find pleasure is not a great option either. Doing so means we will not have a bank of shared, pleasurable memories — for these are the very currency we need to get through trickier times. If we experience most of our pleasurable outlets apart, then we sooner or later turn our relationship into an existence void of shared pleasure. We must enjoy a sizable part of our pleasurable experiences in each other's company. We do not need to love the activity itself; we need only to love seeing our partner happy.

Why do we tolerate living with a non-giggling companion? Is it because our lives may, for the moment, be just comfortable enough to do so?

We tell ourselves that the problem lies elsewhere — that it is not just a compatibility issue. We go to counselling seeking one-sided validation. We fine-tune and edit our true nature in order to make living with a DO companion more tolerable. We invent a more user-friendly avatar version of ourselves that can coexist with our partner's corresponding avatar. We slowly lose touch with our real selves. This continues for as long as we stay within the minimum toleration level. Now that we have removed the functional common necessity to be together, that tolerable level has decreased substantially.

Love relationships can no longer remain in the DO arena. They have very much moved to camp BE. We need to embrace this opportunity. We have to realise that time with our partners needs to be far more about secreting serotonin than adrenalin.

If I am texting my friend, "I'll call you later. Can't talk now. I'm with her," it means I am using adrenalin. This will force me to look for my serotonin elsewhere, not from my partner. If I am editing and censoring my thoughts around my partner in order to keep our relationship going, I need to wake up and realise that I am not with a giggling companion. And a giggling companion is what we need far more than anything else if we wish to enter into a committed relationship with the possibility of having children one day. To do this, we need to interview for a snorting giggler — by snorting and giggling and demonstrating all that makes us giggle. Sharing silliness rather than proving competence is the way forward.

Let us grab this remarkable opportunity to BE happy.

3

WHAT IS LOVE TODAY?

"The unity achieved in productive work is not interpersonal; the unity achieved in orgiastic fusion is transitory; the unity achieved by conformity is only pseudo-unity. Hence, they are only partial answers to the problem of existence. The full answer lies in the achievement of interpersonal union, of fusion with another person, in love."

— Erich Fromm[8]

When it comes to defining love, our views vary considerably. Some prioritise respect and loyalty while others think playfulness and sexual satisfaction are more important. There are those who see love as a barometer for intellectual stimulation, and there are others who see the whole concept as an overrated human preoccupation.

The task becomes even trickier if we try to cater for gender equality, prolonged life expectancy, and insufficient self-awareness. However, I do believe that a better understanding of what love means to us today would help more than we can imagine. I will give a general definition followed by something that is personal to me.

It may help us to think of love as a twin-headed creature with each head unable to survive without the other. The first head is what love means to you. You can design and customise this head however you wish. Find the definition that will make you confidently tell your lover, "To me, love means... And this is why I know I am in love with you."

The second head represents time. Does time keep proving that you are right about your first head? If so, then you still have love. If not, then these heads will fight each other to the bitter end, for they cannot coexist in an environment of pretence. Either the "time head" wins and the relationship ends or the "love head" wins and the honesty in the relationship ends.

I believe time is the missing element from all definitions of love today. Saying "I love you" should be understood as "I love you today," and this should not evoke feelings of insecurity. It's quite the opposite: we should be far more wary of absolute declarations when it comes to matters of the heart. We  need to respect the element of time far more than we do. People grow, and we need to accommodate growth.

Since we have abolished gender roles, there is nothing, functionally speaking, to stop us from leaving our partners. The only thing that can keep us together pleasurably is fulfilment of our emotional needs. Therefore, love needs two components. First, I need to ask whether my partner is fulfilling my emotional needs today and, second, has time increased or decreased my certainty of this feeling?

We need to embrace the idea that love has many stages and not just the initial joyous ones. Living with someone and sharing life's functionalities should prove to us that we have chosen the right partner. Does my partner make my life pleasurable? Or does my life make my partner tolerable? We can never come to a final conclusion; all we can do is allow time to continue to measure our certainty.

Going through the intricacies of real life is exactly what we need to do to determine in which direction our certainty is heading. Therefore, love cannot be seen as a constant, but rather as a variable that changes with time. It is similar to the acquisition of any type of awareness or knowledge: certainty of love takes far longer than we think, and the learning process never really ends.

Because of the immense pleasure derived from the discovery of potential love, we try our hardest to believe that we have discovered a love that will last. We are so desperate to cure our loneliness that we fear honest analysis. We prefer to make early conclusions because *believing* something is true is far easier than *knowing* something is true. That is our nature.

The meaning of love to me:

This is obviously a subjective view and, assuming you don't want to live with me, you can disregard any of the following if you feel it does not apply to you.

To me, love is being with someone who makes you thank your lucky stars every day that you are exactly the way you are. Love is finding the partner who adores your faults and quirks and fears and dramatics — because they are part of the package — and if you begin to trim and edit here and there, you will both lose the wonderful whole. Love is the euphoric joy of being certain about love. Love is realising that you are unconditionally accepted. No, there is no such thing as unconditional. I would like to change that: love is being accepted with the least number of conditions, and the perfect love is when this is reciprocated.

Love is not the excitement of novelty. That is hope.
Love is the euphoria of certainty.

Love is effortlessly feeling joy, inner warmth, and pleasure during the most flawed of our partnership interactions. Think of this scenario: after many years of being together, you find your partner 14 kilograms (30 pounds) heavier, hair growing out of both ears and one nostril, lying on the sofa as you enter the house. The whiff of alcohol implies that your partner was at the pub rather than at the scheduled job interview. Your partner admits to you, "I'm sorry, I really did not want to go for that dull job." If, at that very moment, you can't help but respond to that sheepish smile with a familiar warmth and physical longing, then you know that you hold true love for your partner — the kind of love that Dorothy Tennov describes so accurately as "limerent love."[9]

Limerent love is the invasive, intrusive, yet involuntary act of continually thinking about your lover. Mentally, you are no longer alone. Limerent love takes the choice to love out of your hands. Your only option, as Rumi penned it so eloquently, is to love:

> *"A lover knows only humility, he has no choice.*
> *He steals into your alley at night, he has no choice.*
> *He longs to kiss every lock of your hair, don't fret,*
> *he has no choice.*
> *In his frenzied love for you, he longs to break the*
> *chains of his imprisonment, he has no choice."*[10]

I stand for celebrating love in all its glory. It is what makes us live, breathe, write, sing, feel, explore, try the impossible, evolve, and express to our maximum potential. Having love enables our best qualities to rise to the surface. I hope that we can stigmatise not having it.

Esther Boykin poses the supposition that long-lasting unconditional love is rare because at the early phase of love, we are too drunk from the excitement of finding someone to even begin to substantiate the credibility of our findings. In her article "The Rules of Unconditional Love," she says that "unconditional love is the kind of love that you have for a person not in spite of, but because of their flaws."[11]

The problem here is identified with a genuine intention to help those in need. The advice to help us achieve such love is that we have to establish a set of rules from the start to enable us to deal with the sobriety that comes after the discovery of new-found love.

However, the solution focuses on increasing effort rather than awareness. The partners are expected to be equipped with sufficient awareness and foresight to enable them to put into place rules at the onset, without any guidance.

This assumption gives the lovers far too much credit. The only thing they are sure of is that, at that moment, they are 100 per cent certain of their love. But is that true unconditional love that will pass the trials and tribulations of time? Is what they are feeling lust? Or is it a mixture of love, hope, and lust? Does lust disappear because of the inevitability of the cessation of novelty? Or can lust morph into something far more rewarding if compatibility is there to begin with?

I think words such as commitment, compromise, work, sacrifice, and responsibility are confusing our understanding of love. These are by-products rather than reasons. These are the bonus DO components that, on their own, can no longer sustain a relationship. These words need to be preceded by the phrase "I want to" rather than "I have to": "I want to commit" and "I want to compromise" and "I want to work at it" and "I want to sacrifice" and "I want to be responsible," followed by the phrase "because doing so gives me more joy than I've ever dreamed possible."

Love is insisting that your partner does not change or, at least, continues to explore freely the journey of self-discovery. Love means having no secrets. You should be able to admit to anything: "I was caught drinking and driving," "I think I fancy my daughter's boyfriend," "I tried cocaine last night," "I used my vibrator in a new way," or "I am not declaring all my income to avoid tax." You should feel extremely comfortable sharing such information with your love because you know that the reaction will be forgiving, non-judgemental, comforting, or even playful where the interest is in sharing rather than judging.

In the bedroom, how many of us would dare say to our partners, "Shhh. I'm thinking of my gym instructor," confident that the response would be, "I love your brain," because your partner knows that what you are really saying is, "You are the one with whom I have no inhibitions, the one with whom I want to be the most honest, the one with whom I don't fear sharing all my thoughts. You are the one with whom I want to share my most intimate, perverted, scary, euphoric, sadistic, orgasmic, depressing, evil, and liberating thoughts. With you, I can be my true self because you are 'the one.'" Then, and only then, can that hope of love move closer to certainty.

When it comes to choosing, we need to believe that we have found "the one." I know there is no such thing as "the only one," but feeling as if that one person is uniquely "the one" is a wonderful basis upon which to start your relationship. This will not guarantee eternal bliss. However, start because you believe you are with "the one," and you have hope; start for any other reason, and you will significantly increase your chances of swimming in that sea of lovelessness.

So why do we tolerate starting or staying with someone whom we cannot classify as "the one"?

4

WHY DO WE TOLERATE NOT HAVING LOVE?

"The source of all pleasure and delight is the feeling of kinship. Even with the sense of beauty, it is unquestionably our own species in the animal world, and then again our own race, that appears to us the fairest. So, too, in intercourse with others, every man shows a decided preference for those who resemble him."

— *Arthur Schopenhauer*[12]

In one of my recent seminars, I asked for "three words that you associate with marriage." The top five answers were children, home, stability, commitment, and security. The words "fun" and "pleasure" were not even mentioned. We tend to accept partnership incompatibility by viewing long-term love as an exercise of mature compromise. We convince ourselves that it takes "hard work" to keep love alive.

I agree that relationships do involve hard work, but that is not because relationships are hard; it is because life is. We need to work and pay the rent regardless, so why not do it with someone fun, someone compatible? The problem is we have somehow reasoned convincingly that incompatibility can be advantageous through the widely accepted principle that "opposites attract." Why is that?

Evolution taught us to tolerate

Evolution ensured that the fittest who survived were those who "stuck together," those who came back to the safety of a cave occupied by a known mate. We use these hardwired, built-in mechanisms in our relationships today. We refuse to give up on a partner and consequently find reasons to re-examine, justify, and persevere. We do not question whether or not our partner is compatible with us. We instead ask, "What can we do to make this partnership work better in order to preserve the safety of our cave?"

In the majority of cases, however, our cave is no longer the safe and welcoming haven it is supposed to be. The cave is not facilitating relaxation and acceptance of who we are. The cave needs us to DO: to perform functions not because we want to, but rather to avoid aggravation, to minimise pain, and to avoid being reprimanded, openly or tacitly, by our partners.

Think of your front door. Do you find it more liberating to enter it or to exit it?

Another reason for putting up with incompatibility is the evolutionary blindfold. In her book *Love and Limerence: The Experience of Being in Love*, Dorothy Tennov explains that the infatuation phase of discovering a lover blinds us for eighteen months to three years.[13] This blindfold allows time for the woman to get pregnant and give birth and for the child to develop independence. Once the child can fend for itself, the parents become less duty-bound to be together. In other words, we really do see each other through rose-tinted glasses for up to three years.

The children of the couples that stay together during that initial phase are more likely to survive. Through Darwinian natural selection, the parental tendency to put the child's early nurturing needs first has survived.

After millions of years of this behaviour, the blindfolding mechanism is very much a part of our make-up, and we probably do not selfishly, or accurately, evaluate relationships until some time has passed. Therefore, it makes perfect sense for us to live in incompatibility tolerance during the initial phase of a relationship.

By the time we remove the rose-tinted glasses and evaluate the partnership, the exit strategies that are available become less attractive — particularly if we now have children and have invested together in a house. This may lead us to opt for the comfortable illusion of a happy partnership. It seems prudent to convey an image of happy commitment and not to follow our hearts.

It is in the interest of all

Historically, a marriage breakdown negatively affects the interests of many, not just the couple. It is only natural that society, with its best intentions, encourages the couple to learn to tolerate their differences. A friend might meet your partner and think, *OMG! You're such fun, and he's so dull. How the hell do you put up with each other?* In reality, your friend will probably say, "He seems very kind, a bit quiet, but you probably need someone like that to ground you," or "You two complement each other well because you're so different," or "You're bound to get on each other's nerves at the start. In time, you'll learn to accept your differences."

These are the mechanisms we all put into place to protect the union of the couple.

This makes historical sense because marriage was traditionally a union of two people from different families, tribes, or communities who would become connected by common interests. The success or failure of the marriage reflected on, and affected, the greater community. How necessary this built-in protectionist behaviour is in the twenty-first century, especially within modern liberal societies, is up for debate.

Perhaps more relevant advice should be: "If you're not happy, do something about it. You have only one life to live." Caring friends and family are more honest these days, which may be a factor contributing to increased rates of separation and divorce. Nevertheless, protectionist default reactions are still hardwired within us.

We use intelligence to justify it

Intelligence helps us put up with an incompatible partnership. We learn what to say and what to keep inside. We learn that saying, "I don't want to see your friend and his wife because I don't like them" is not the right way to express this sentiment. Instead, we say, "Oh no, what a shame we can't do it that day because I think we have a prior engagement," or "I'd love to, but I really don't feel well. I think I've come down with something. Why don't you go without me?" In short, we learn to minimise pain.

We cleverly create personas that are versions of our true selves so that we can better "communicate" with our partners or, rather, our partners' corresponding personas. We have developed this skill over millions of years, ever since we evolved from a solitary to a social animal. These are the skills needed to sustain DO relationships. We therefore find it easier to use these skills in our love relationships rather than confront the problem that is causing us to resort to using such skills.

Familiarity and fear of the unknown

As creatures of habit, we prefer to put up with what we know. The uncertainty of what we *could have* leads us to overvalue what we *do have*. If we are comfortable, we tend to let things go. We fear being alone, and we fear the prospect of starting the search again. We try to tell ourselves, "I'm not uncomfortable in my current relationship. I'm not happy, the butterflies have gone, but why rock the boat?" This attitude changes if either our comfortable, acceptable, minimum safety level is compromised, or if we allow ourselves to become aware of the alternatives that offer tangible hope.

If our safety is compromised, we seriously consider, and often do, end up leaving partnerships. A parent is more likely to take the children and leave if the partner is abusive. Even illness or financial instability can increase the likelihood of separation.

In America, the divorce rate in marriages where there is a chronic illness is more than 75 per cent.[14] Financial difficulties or disagreements also greatly increase the risk of divorce.[15]

Another scenario that decreases the fear of the unknown is finding new love. In the United States, new relationships account for a 20 per cent increase in the divorce rate.[16] Finding new love, with the chance of experiencing true happiness, makes the future less intimidating and gives us reason, courage, and justification to leave our DO relationships.

I believe that affairs are cries for help from our hearts. Finding new love gives us the courage to try again. But the way ahead, once new love is found, is fraught with danger — especially when children are involved. If we realise that our hearts are back in search mode, what we should do, ideally, is to be honest and acknowledge this to ourselves long before finding new love and before we start families.

We blame it on life's luggage

We are masters of shifting blame. We may reason, for example, that personal repressed issues are to blame for our relationship difficulties. We decide to deal with these repressed issues in order to communicate better with our partners. Even though there may be an element of truth in this reasoning, it is masking the real issue.

We all come with luggage. The point is to find someone who will love us in our entirety, luggage and all. I am not saying that it is our partner's job to resolve our issues, but it is a partner's job to accept the luggage as part of a wonderful whole.

We blame incompatibility on the unresolved issues we may have accumulated over the years: "My relationship is suffering because I have mother issues." "As an only child, I have problems communicating, and my relationship is suffering because of this." "I have an issue with confrontation because my parents loved me for what I did, not who I was." "I have a problem relaxing, and that can be overwhelming for my partner."

Yes, we have each travelled on our own unique journey, but why should this be an obstacle to a happy relationship? Why can't this be a journey of self-discovery? We are here, we have issues, or rather we have discovered how we feel about certain things through experiences. These experiences have brought us to where we are today. Why can't we just look for someone who finds our current selves to be endearing, soothing, funny, admirable, caring, attractive, and sexy. In other words, "compatible"?

Shouldn't we continue to search for someone who unconditionally accepts us for who we are today, not one who hopes that one day we will be more compatible once we have dealt with our issues?

I highly recommend self-therapy to increase self-awareness. Couples therapy to find out how partners can "tolerate" each other is wrong on so many levels. This is not love — it is lobotomy. (The exception, of course, is if a relationship may be suffering not because of incompatibility, but rather because of external issues such as abuse or addiction. If this is the case, immediate professional guidance is the way forward.)

It is worth considering that by finding someone who likes the fact that you are so impatient, or that you cannot get along with your parents, or that you would rather not talk in the morning, or that you enjoy talking during sex, you may become more accepting and forgiving of yourself to a point where you may even begin to like yourself. This, in turn, may help you become more forgiving and accepting of others.

These could be the very issues that, if your partner judges to be irritating, eventually lead you to seek couples therapy. If, however, your mother asks your partner, "How the hell do you cope with her morning silence?" and your partner answers, "That's one of the many things I love about her," your partnership is strengthened, you feel happier, you don't need to justify or validate, and you get a little bit further on your self-acceptance journey.

So life's luggage is really just a way of finding out about yourself. If the survival of your relationship with your partner depends on altering or controlling or dealing with who you are, luggage and all — to the point where you seek therapy — then surely the wrong is not with you. The problem lies in your partner's perception of you.

We confuse monogamy with love

You will find many fine professions that "we cannot be together for a long time because we are not meant to be monogamous." This is a classic reason to excuse a problematic relationship. We find it logical to agree that monogamy leads to boredom and that the strong and righteous tolerate boredom, whereas the weak and wicked allow boredom to lead to infidelity and, in turn, infidelity leads to relationship disharmony. This offers a powerful and universally acceptable explanation that pins the fault of disharmony firmly on the symptoms rather than the cause of the problem.

Our understanding of sex and love is changing. We are becoming honest enough to acknowledge that monogamy does not mean love and that love does not require monogamy as a prerequisite.

This is highlighted in Meghan Laslocky's *The Little Book of Heartbreak: Love Gone Wrong Through the Ages.*[17] She argues that monogamy is a man-made concept put into place to ensure offspring legitimacy but has no biological logic. Of the four thousand mammals in the animal kingdom, less than 3 per cent are monogamous, and even the monogamy of that 3 per cent is purely a human projection.

Take the perception of lovebirds as being monogamous. It was discovered that, if observed over time, at least one of the partners will be found entertaining another lovebird on the side.

The monogamy that exists in the animal kingdom, she argues, is what is known as "social monogamy" in which the aim is to be together during the child-nurturing phase, rather than be sexually faithful. This does not stop either partner from experiencing sexual encounters with others. In fact, the scientific view is that promiscuity benefits the procreation of the species and increases the support network available to the females during the nurturing phase. Because the father's identity is not guaranteed, more than one male can be found to be offering help.

We may be reaching a point where we can begin to reconsider our views on monogamy. However, even if we agree that we are not naturally monogamous, it does not mean that we cannot cohabit happily with continuous pleasure for a long period. Here is where our current relationship understanding does not allow us to see pleasurable cohabitation and monogamy as separate entities.

Sex and love are different commodities. We can get addicted to a person irrespective of the frequency or proficiency of our sexual interactions. A study carried out at Berkeley University based on Laslocky's book shows that being in love with someone is, in essence, an addiction. We can experience and enjoy work, hobbies, and sexual activities with others without affecting the good feeling that our true BE love gives us. That precious high can be derived from only one source, one person — the person we truly love.[18]

We get addicted to that love as we do to any other addictive substance. The same areas and mechanisms of our brain come into play.

You can stay in love with someone for a lifetime, but the relationship is not reliant on monogamy. In other words, monogamy does not lead to the continuation or the cessation of true love. We simply hypothesise, erroneously, that promiscuity means, or leads to, loss of love.

We need to be compatible, serotonin-inducing co-gigglers to discuss this topic openly and honestly. We cannot entertain the idea that promiscuity can exist in a happy long-term relationship because our relationship values are derived from a DO way of thinking.

From the early days of cohabitation, the female's main purpose was to give birth to her partner's children. Thankfully, we now see women differently. I hope we are now beginning to see that our partnerships need to become serotonin-inducing BE companionships, and that this must acquire a higher priority than being monogamous or promiscuous.

Our cups are being filled elsewhere

Imagine that each of us has three cups of love inside ourselves: a Childhood, a Self, and an Adulthood Cup of love. These cups get filled whenever we are positively acknowledged or, if you prefer, validated, for being who we are. Only BE relationship interactions can fill these cups.

The Three Cups of love

Childhood

Self

Picture these cups arranged so that Childhood is slightly above Self, which is slightly above Adulthood. If a Childhood Cup is overflowing, then it will spill into the Self Cup, and similarly from the Self to the Adulthood Cup. However, the reverse route is not possible. With that picture in mind, let us look at each cup.

Adulthood

The Childhood Cup, the nurturing cup, is filled by our caregivers, be it parents or the parental figures in our lives.

How much did they make us believe that they loved us unconditionally, and how much of it was judgemental? Was it a

BE love or a DO love? Did we feel they loved us for who we were (BE) or for what we did in terms of our usefulness (DO)?

If a child misbehaves and the parent's reaction to this misbehaviour is "That was a silly thing to do, but I know you won't do it again. Come and give me a hug," then that child's Childhood Cup is topped up a bit. Similarly, if a parent responds to a bad grade at school with concern, comfort, love, and a dialogue to identify support mechanisms to improve the grade, then that child feels loved. The child will understand that doing well does not define a parent's love and that achieving is a good thing, but it has zero effect on the parental love.

Conversely, if a parent's reaction to a bad grade leaves the child feeling isolated and rejected, with low self-esteem, then the Childhood Cup will not be topped up. It will instead be reduced.

Caregivers may be acting with all the right intentions. Perhaps the parents are projecting their own fears of limited opportunities for those who do not achieve success in their education. If they deny love when achievement is low and give love when grades are good, then they do not top up the cup because the love is for the grade, not for the child. The Childhood Cup full of love and self-worth is symbolic of a BE child-parent relationship.

In *The Loveless Family*, Jon P. Bloch tells us that if children do not experience love from their parents, they will be unable to love their own families in the future.[19] Unloved children grow up to be adults who are incapable of demanding BE love from their partners, and if they are not receiving it, they will feel that the fault is theirs. They see a relationship problem as a sole responsibility rather than a joint relationship issue.

Low or empty Childhood Cup children feel that everything they do is judged, which leads to low self-esteem and an inability to respond to criticism. If, on the other hand, we have self-worth, we say, "This is who I am, and that is who you are. Do we love enough of each other as we are to have a committed relationship?" Without self-worth, we tend to avoid confrontation, blame ourselves, or live in denial, all under an illusion of love.

If our Childhood Cup is full, we have the confidence to investigate the health of our adult relationships — even if it means having to face unpleasant realities.

I believe that parents who have true love find it easier to fill their children's Childhood Cups.

The second cup, the Self Cup, tells us whether we are happy with ourselves. Our characters, careers, ambitions, hobbies, realised dreams, children, and personal health are the types of sources that determine this cup. How happy are we with who we are? Do we allow ourselves to indulge in pleasures, fantasies, and dreams? Whether it is a yes or a no, is this something that makes us inwardly happy, or do we wish it could be different?

The level of our Childhood Cup has a great effect on our Self Cup. If our Childhood Cup is full, we are more likely to seek out rewarding sources to fill our Self Cup. Even if these sources have a low probability of success, we will opt for such rewarding pursuits because if we fail, we still have one full cup.

If the Childhood Cup is empty, we may opt for a guarantee of filling the Self Cup to avoid having two empty cups. I may want to be a rock star but feel that it is overindulgent of me to pursue such a risky path; therefore, I instead opt for a career in law. I may justify this by saying that I need to be responsible and ensure I become self-sufficient rather than be a burden on or a disappointment to anyone.

Of course I am not blaming a child's inability to succeed or to pursue dreams solely on unloving parents. Some young people do succeed in spite of lack of parental love — possibly because of nonparental influences around them. Others don't try, even with an abundance of parental love. In such circumstances, closer observation may reveal that outside influences, such as peers or mentors, may have filled or depleted the Childhood or Self Cups.

What does all this analysis of inner cups have to do with compatibility and love in a relationship? I am trying to point out core personality differences that determine our inner beliefs and decision-making systems. These core differences affect our day-to-day interactions with our partners. They affect even the simplest of decisions, such as the way we plan a trip to the cinema: "Should we leave early to find a parking space or take our time and hope for the best?" If we are in relationships with people with whom we have so many of these differences, irritation can accumulate significantly.

The same applies to career choices, attitudes toward money, risk averseness, morning moods, and many other aspects of our lives.

My concern is that ignoring such different personality attributes leads to the pairing of incompatibles. The partners will ignore their differences at the start, or even see them as quirky because of their novelty, and believe in the fallacy that "opposites attract." That hope eventually dissolves as the taxing management of incompatibility chips away at love and admiration.

Adult BE relationships fill the Adulthood Cup. Historically, surrounding communities greatly contributed to the filling of this cup from many sources. As we gained independence from the community and acquired the freedoms of individualism, other sources, such as relatives, village elders and local figures of authority became negligible. The main, if not only, source for the Adulthood Cup of love takes the form of the life partner.

If your partner effortlessly expresses love and admiration of your instinctive thoughts and behaviours, no matter how flawed others may perceive them to be, your Adulthood Cup is incremented. If, however, you receive criticism from your partner for what seems to you as simply being yourself, then your cup will be reduced.

Now let us further consider the concept of the minimal tolerance level. Let us set this at one and one-half out of three cups. Therefore, the necessity to fill the Adulthood Cup is very much dependent on the levels of the first two cups. If we have unconditional love from our caregivers and we are self-fulfilled in our careers and hobbies and interests to a point where our

Childhood and Self Cups are full and could be overflowing into the Adulthood Cup, the fact that our partner is not filling our Adulthood Cup becomes far more tolerable.

You find yourself saying: "As long as we both play our roles, buy the Valentine's Day cards, show our faces on social occasions, share the household chores, then we can get on with it and avoid complicating our lives."

The problem surfaces when the filling of the Self Cup starts to slow down to a point where it can no longer overflow into the Adulthood Cup. This could happen if, for example, our careers suffer to a point where social status and financial comfort are affected. What then? What if illness befalls a partnership? What if children, who may have been a source of filling the Self Cup, grow up and start their own lives? If such turns of events lead to the cessation of cup filling, then the total level eventually will fall below the tolerable minimum, and that is when incompatibility is difficult to tolerate.

Sometimes the relationship may be so incompatible that our Adulthood Cup needs to borrow from the Self Cup to stop it from going into a negative. If we are borrowing from the Self Cup at a faster rate than the Self Cup is being filled, then the total eventually falls below the minimum level and toleration becomes intolerable.

A thought worth considering is that, as individualism increases, perhaps the size of our Adulthood Cup will also increase and become larger than the first two cups, thus making the minimum 50 per cent far more dependent on the Adulthood Cup.

It could be that this is already happening, which may explain the many separations of people who, on the face of it, seem to be comfortable and fulfilled in their personal and work lives but have different realities.

Unfortunately, divorce is an option

We have the get-out clause of divorce to end incompatible and intolerable relationships. We may therefore ask: why do we need a new system?

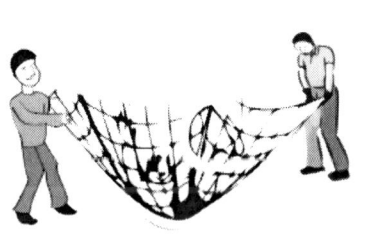

I believe that divorce is a difficult and damaging exit strategy. To me, divorce is the net we place under trapeze artists. We send these artists up ladders to perform their routines without any proper training. As they begin to fall, the safety nets soften the landing. As the falls increase, we come up with better and stronger nets, such as prenuptial agreements. However, we never consider that what these "wannabe" acrobats need is better training before they go up and continual assessment to determine whether they are still fit and able to follow their dreams.

The safety nets may cushion the fall, but they do not compensate for the time wasted to go up the ladder, the missed opportunity to enjoy the full pleasures of being a trapeze artist and, not least, the pessimism acquired as a result of disillusionment. The answer surely is better training and continual assessment so that we can maximise the pleasure, not just minimise the pain.

We tell ourselves that divorce is better for the children in the long run. The truth is that, given the choice, children would always prefer happy parents and stable homes. Divorce does not bring us or our children pleasure. At best, it serves only to minimise the pain while recovering from the breakdown. We somehow use divorce to try to reach a place of lesser pain, but not zero pain and maximised pleasure.

Watching our children suffer the trauma of parental separation and feeling the dilution of our relationship with them does not belong in the realm of pleasure.

We need to train and assess these trapeze artists better so that we can stop them from ascending the ropes if they are not ready. Even if we drastically lower the number of those who fall through better training, we still need a better exit strategy than divorce for those who may fall.

Divorce is like an expensive insurance policy to help us rebuild our home after a destructive hurricane. It does not identify nor tackle the weakness in the foundation that has led to the collapse of our house.

* * *

As Bloch says,

"Home is where we love."[20]

As far as modern man is concerned, our partner's main purpose is to liberate our inhibitions, to maximise our courage, to dare us to dream, and to maintain belief in us when we fail.

We need to promote the beauty of least conditionally* accepting love and the infinite benefits it brings. Such love must be a prerequisite for cohabiting.

---

* In reality, there is no such thing as unconditional love. There will always be some differences of opinion. Therefore when choosing a life partner, what we need to ask is this: who loves me with the least number of conditions?

5

HOW DO I FIND MY COMPATIBLE PARTNER?

Books offering relationship advice are a dime a dozen. The majority of them, however, deal with problems that arise as the relationship matures. You will struggle to find literature that advises couples to recognise incompatibility at the start of their relationships.

You need to ask the question: "How do I know that I am beginning a relationship with the right partner?" The answer currently is: "You will know when you are in love. You will feel it." Does that mean that the 50 per cent who get divorced go ahead with a marriage even though they know they are not in love?

If we ask divorcees, "Looking back, were there warning signs before you got married and, if there were, did you ignore them?" The majority would answer, "Yes."[21]

Our relationships need to take a page out of our platonic-friendship handbook. In a platonic friendship, we make more honest judgements and adjust the levels of contact and communication accordingly. In a relationship, we may try too hard and tolerate too much in the hope that things will improve.

Gauge your compatibility account

View compatibility as a scale from "extremely judgemental" to "unconditionally accepting." The person of the preferred sex who is closest to the "unconditionally accepting" end of the scale has the highest chance of becoming a lasting compatible partner with whom, for the most part, we will agree rather than disagree.

By "agree," I do not mean that both prefer red meat to chicken or sports to art. "Agree" means that when we express ourselves instinctively and honestly, we receive acceptance, not accusations or mistrust.

To define the compatibility account, picture yourself sharing a joint account with everyone you know. If you know one hundred people, then you have one hundred joint accounts.

If I feel that my level of happiness in my relationship is low, then so does my partner. I cannot say that I am unhappy, but she is happy because she buys a handbag every other week and I pay for it. The real measure of our joint account is not in the number of handbags or golfing vacations; it is in the pleasure derived from being together. Everything else is a source that does not fill the Adulthood Cup.

At the start of any relationship, we open a joint compatibility account. We both immediately receive credit into this account purely through the joy of the novelty and the hope for happiness. Let us say we are initially credited with one hundred compatibility units.

As time goes by, the account balance either increases or decreases. An irritation debits the account, and a pleasurable interaction credits it. Let us say that a certain irritation debits the account by five units. At the start, this is affordable. If, after some time, the balance reaches a low level, that same irritation becomes far less tolerable and could lead to acrimony.

Increase in effortlessly being yourself =
Increase in the compatibility account.
Increase in relationship management skills =
Decrease in the compatibility account.

As an account balance increases, the friendship moves to the next level on the BE friendship line. The love partner should be seen as the last stop on this line.

The BE friendship line:

Stranger — Someone we know — Friend — Good friend —
Close friend — Love partner

Becoming a close friend takes time and many shared experiences and emotions. We cannot, and should not, skip any of the steps or speed up a friendship's natural pace.

For love to survive and be the primary reason for a long-term relationship, we must rethink our understanding of the love partner.

We are moving along the friendship line — the line that takes into account all of the people with whom you have become acquainted, many who will disappear or stay at the early stages of the friendship line. Very few make it to the latter stages. The partner you choose should come from within the small group of close friends.

Some may ask, "What if I'm not attracted to any of my close friends?" Choosing an incompatible attractive partner may lead to sexual pleasure, but the likelihood that this pleasure will last is low.

Compatibility should be physical and mental. If you do not find any of your close friends attractive and you do not consider any of your attractive friends close, all that means is that you haven't yet met a compatible partner. It maybe that you prefer an alternative lifestyle to coupling. Living with another is no longer the only socially acceptable way of life and therefore you must not choose the best available option just so you can enter the kingdom of coupledom.

Cohabiting with someone incompatible results in wasted energy. You should spend this energy getting to know yourself better so you can find the person who will fill your Adulthood Cup and, eventually, your children's Childhood Cups.

The birth of a child can have enormous consequences on a relationship. Research shows that for many couples, sex and intimacy decrease substantially after the birth of a child.[22] Why is that? Is it that the introduction of a child reduces the opportunities for pleasures outside the partnership such as hobbies or socialising — the ones that have been filling our Self Cup outside the partnership? Or could it be that our compatibility account with our partner is so low that our visceral reaction to the birth of our child is to shift all our emotional investment from the illusionary love (the incompatible partner) to the genuine love (our newborn child)? What could be better than children to give us hope of redemption and validation?

Compatibility Account with Our Children

Our love for our newborn children is unconditional — we hold no compatibility accounts for them. We see them as a "work in progress," a personal and fulfilling one that is a source for filling our Self Cup.

When a child becomes old enough to question, to criticise, and to answer back, our compatibility account with our child opens and we begin to judge each other. They no longer unquestioningly validate us.

This is when we need to treat our child as a newly-found friend in order to nourish our mutual love and joy. Although we must never forget the importance of our role as a caregiver, we must honestly reveal our thoughts, weaknesses, pleasures, and dreams and encourage them to reciprocate. A friendship begins.

Take your time

There is no substitute for time. Its passage will tell you whether passion turns to duty and whether a functional existence replaces joy. Constantly and honestly assess whether or not the passion of body and soul that first attracted you to each other is still present, even allowing for the functionalities of life.

Remember not to confuse the comfort of a DO relationship with the exhilarating love of a BE relationship. The latter relationship triggers laughter as well as sexual, sensual, and mental orgasms that can transcend all difficulties.

Do you maximise pleasure or minimise pain within your relationship?

Throughout our partnership, we need to ask, "Are we maximising pleasure or minimising pain?" Do you call your partner because of an expectation or because you love the sound of your partner's voice?

Look at the sources of your pleasure. Do most of them emanate from interactions with your partner or from interactions with others?

Look, too, at the daily transactions with your partner. Of course, many will be mundane and functional. But are they executed in enjoyable, serotonin-inducing ways? If you have more adrenaline moments, you need to address issues before you make further commitments.

Have you conquered your sexual watchdog?

"Today, our sexuality is an open-ended personal project; it is part of who we are, an identity, and no longer merely something we do. It has become a central feature of intimate relationships, and sexual satisfaction, we believe, is our due. The era of pleasure has arrived."

— Esther Perel[23]

What could be more romantic than knowing that you and your partner have chosen each other for the reasons of pure love and pleasure and hope to continue to choose each other every day?

Freedom of expression in the bedroom is a telling gauge for measuring the serotonin in a relationship.

Any form of activity — whether it is playing tennis, cooking together, engaging in meaningful conversations, or having sex — should be joyful and liberating. We should partake in sexual activities without fear of reproach and express ourselves freely and openly, not using our sexual watchdog to monitor what we can or cannot disclose.

We risk forgetting that sex is adult play, and the very nature of play is that it is imaginative, creative, ludicrous, silly, and reckless. Sex should be a serotonin-inducing exercise. We do not want to place it in the realm of duty with our minds "focusing on the task at hand." We need to openly share our fantasies and our weird and wonderful sexual thoughts with our partners.

We need to find out about each other's sexuality, right from the beginning, to help us understand each other's levels of risk, perceptions of right and wrong, sources of pleasure, and what constitutes acceptable naughtiness. Otherwise, we are in danger of sharing more of our fantasies with our friends than with our lovers.

There is nothing healthier than an ongoing, free, non-judgemental dialogue between partners who can discuss fantasies and, in a BE relationship, act upon those fantasies with no fear on either side of lack of respect, love, or loss of total commitment.

It does not matter what your preferred game is. It may be a threesome or indulging in pornography. It is up to you, your partner, and your freely roaming brains. There is a whole world out there that is a long way from the missionary position every other Wednesday while fantasising over some fading image stored in the emergency memory bank.

"I'm always with you in mind and spirit and sexual thought." Imagine how good it would feel to be able to say such words and mean them. Why don't we dare to think like that? Why is it that we cannot address our need to feel chosen every day, not because of some piece of paper we have signed?

When it comes to sex and most other playful pleasures, the journey from erotic excitement to "I can't be bothered to make an effort" does not happen overnight. Slowly, you give up and begin to fill your cups elsewhere through work, family, children, affairs, or hobbies. Why does that happen with most couples and only very few manage to stay honest, childish, adventurous, and true in thought?

Sexual play and freedom of expression are metaphors for the liberation of thought. There is only one rule to follow, and that is to be uncompromisingly honest. Face the fact that you both have wondering brains. You will be approached, and your eyes will roam. Share such thoughts and experiences with your partner from day one, before a pattern of non-disclosure sets in. See whether this disclosure reassures both of you and elevates you to greater joy and intimacy, or whether it leads to greater insecurity.

If you have not reached this level of understanding, your sexual watchdog will have to screen any flirtations with perverse thoughts or interactions that may cause a tingle in your libido. You end up waiting for your sexual watchdog's permission before you reveal such thoughts to your partner. Such screening can crush the intended joy.

So much resentment builds up when we do not disclose our fantasies and sexual needs. This does not allow the friendship to move forward. After time, any disclosure or fantasy suggestion may result only in increasing insecurities and lowering the level of love.

Sharing sexual fantasies, from day one, is an excellent test of compatibility. Let your mind naturally demonstrate that the rest of the world and all its offerings are but a mere collection of props in your play, with you and your partner as the lead characters.

If sharing sexual thoughts and experiences honestly and truthfully leads to joint pleasure, then maybe your partner is the one with whom you can live and maintain long-lasting happiness.

Some Lateral Thinking

Telling your partner about your fantasies and sexual experiences, past and present, long before you even think about having children, is the kindest thing you can do for your children.

Mischief sharing with, and probably even more important, mischief disclosure to, a partner will make you better parents. Many of us believe that we do not need to share everything with our partners. For example, you engaged in sexual experiences during your youth. It was fun at the time, but you would not want to do it again, so why tell your partner about it? Why cause unwanted judgements or insecurities because of something that you did once and are unlikely to do again?

This is fine if you have no intention of having children with this partner. It is not if you have such intention.

Let us say you do not reveal these sexual experiences, and years later your child has a similar experience. Your partner cannot fathom why your child would do something so crass, vulgar, and unacceptable. You, on the other hand, may react by saying, "Sweetheart, aren't you overreacting? We were all young once," and this "sweetheart" replies, "What is wrong with you? I can't believe you're OK with this. This is your fault. You encourage this behaviour without even knowing it." And we can all guess how such enjoyable exchanges go from there.

I use sexual experience as an example. It could be any life experience such as stealing sweets from a shop, swearing, watching pornography, or trying recreational drugs. Parents need to be of one mind in their child's eyes. It is important that children perceive their parents as close friends who agree far more than they disagree.

Let us say that one parent finds out about a certain incident before the other. The child does not want to see Dad worried about what Mum thinks of Dad's advice or vice versa. They definitely do not want to hear Mum saying, "What you did isn't that bad, my love. This is what being young is all about. Don't be so hard on yourself," when Dad's reaction is, "How could you? I'm so disappointed. I don't want to talk to you for a month, and you are grounded for three."

If you wish to portray your views and beliefs to your child, you want to count on your partner's automatic support for the vast majority of the time. Therefore, if you want to be part of a shining example of a loving, happy, united couple to your children, rather than a fearful, emotionally challenged, gutless, fence-sitting partner who finds yourself thinking, *I had better not react until I see what my partner does because the last thing I want is to have a fight or be told off, again, or I had better deal with this now before my partner returns and ruins all my good work by unpredictable input,* then revealing all of your sexual experiences and fantasies from the beginning of your relationship is the way forward.

Therefore, sharing mischievous experiences with, and revealing our individual mischievous stories to, our partners will affect the well-being of our children.

It will provide insight into our respective views on character-defining subjects such as politeness, sexual adventure, level of frankness, and level of acceptable human fallibility that we wish to pass to our children.

Stress will have a far higher chance of being replaced by joy if we have our partners' unconditional support most of the time.

Refuse to conform; we are all unique

I cannot understand why so many couples compare their own relationships with others: "Can you see Mary saying that to her husband?" or "Eddie wouldn't dare treat his wife that way. He spoils her rotten." What Mary and Eddie do with their respective partners is their own business. If it works for them, great, but it does not mean it will work for you. Besides, no one knows what really goes on behind closed doors.

Moreover, your journey to this point of your life, and of your partnership, is not identical to Eddie's or Mary's or anyone else's.

Therefore, the only comparing that should be of your concern is how you feel now about each other compared with how you felt before. Have you met, exceeded, or fallen short of your original expectations?

By comparing yourself with others, what you are really saying is:

I don't really love you anymore. I have discovered that my assessment of our love was wrong. Had I known back then what I know now, had I put real effort into finding out if we, as people, truly ring each other's bells, then, more than likely, I would not have decided to live with you this long. I had my doubts, but I didn't take them seriously, and here we are now.

For some temporary relief, I will now and then find opportunities to show you how disappointed I am. Comparing us with others is just one way of showing you this disappointment.

Deep down, I know this is not right. But somehow I find it less frightening to tolerate than to actively seek change.

Having considered all of the above, I think the best solution for us is to continue in our comfortable illusion that is similar to so many of our equally dissatisfied peers, and which will be acceptable to our friends and family.

Comparing with others does not help us in any way. At best, it provides momentary comfort to our pain.

Speak the bubble above your head

Most of our relationships are DO relationships. Our relationships with our work colleagues, doctors, neighbours, local bakers, and many others exist because of a common functional goal. Within the context of a DO relationship, it is highly advisable and perfectly understandable to think before we speak. This does not apply to BE relationships. In reality, telling our partners exactly what is on our minds is what we should be doing.

Once we begin to filter and censor what we say, pain minimising replaces pleasure maximising. Why don't couples speak the truth? "During sex, I was thinking of our son's math teacher." What is wrong with that statement? We would readily tell our friends that such a thought crossed our minds with the hope of sharing a giggle. "This weekend, I really don't want to see your parents again." "No, I don't think we need a new car. I'd rather go on holiday." "I was fantasising about sitting on the gardener's face." "Look at that waiter. Now that's what I call hot." "How do you feel about a threesome?" "I watch porn on the Internet at least three times a week." "Cutting your hair shorter would make zero difference to how I feel about you, but oral sex might."

I am, perhaps, pushing the limits here to make a point, but why not? When I am with my partner, I want to be my real self. I want to be free to express every single thought in my head without censorship of any form. I want to say what I am thinking because that is the real me, and I want to know whether my partner loves the real me.

If speaking the truth leads to my partner's honesty, and this gives us both pleasure, then I have found my "happy cave." If it leads to argument, fear, and rejection, then at least we know where we are.

No partnership can score 100 per cent. The question is: with whom do we speak our bubble the most? Is it with our partner? If not, we need to find out why and see whether we can change this. If we cannot, we need to consider the possibility that we are not compatible.

We show far less fear in sharing so many intimate thoughts with our friends, yet we argue that by doing this with a partner from the beginning, we may well jeopardise the relationship.

We need to realise that the most effective technique for gauging a partnership's true level of compatibility is the sharing of genuine thoughts, no matter how silly, funny, sinister, or perverted, as and when they form in the thought bubbles above our heads. *In particular, the thoughts that we must share are the very ones we currently withhold for fear of judgement or rejection.*

Look at the example in the sketch. He wants to find out whether she is dull, and she needs to know whether she is just another on a conveyor belt of dates. How and what words they choose to express these sentiments is irrelevant. The point is to share the truth. He can say something along the lines of, "I know this is silly, but I try hard not to use the word 'nice.' I don't know why," and she can say, "Is this your favourite place for dates?" These opening lines express what they are actually thinking. This will give their level of compatibility a chance to reveal itself. Does sharing actual thoughts lead to serotonin-inducing pleasurable exchanges? If so, you're going in the right direction.

Learning to exchange genuine thoughts is extremely underrated in current relationship communication. The goal is to see if sharing real thoughts, especially those we've been conditioned to avoid sharing, leads to a positive pleasurable reaction or to awkwardness and rejection. If it's the former, we not only move closer to finding potential compatible partners, but we also take leaps forward in our own self-awareness journeys. This, in effect, is self-therapy by love.

If the two in our sketch share their actual thoughts, they have a chance of exploring why they have certain fears and anxieties. If this leads both to say, "I get where you're coming from; in fact, I'm like that, too," and mean it, they will feel more hopeful about finding love. In doing so, they will get to know *and* accept themselves a little bit more. True love and self-awareness grow hand in hand.

We must ensure that by the time we are ready to commit long term, formality and editing have all but disappeared and been replaced by effortless sharing of inner thoughts.

Currently, such serotonin-filled partnerships get there through hefty doses of luck. I hope that one day they become the norm through better awareness and an acknowledgement that we need to change our understandings of partnerships.

With partners, we need to speak the bubble from minute one.

Let us not confuse love with sex

Love and sex are far less related than we think. In her book *Why Him? Why Her?* Helen Fisher demonstrates how sexual attraction is activated by completely separate chemical reactions in different parts of the brain than those associated with long-term love.[24]

You can achieve sexual arousal in an instant with a complete stranger, but you cannot fall in love with that stranger. After time, however, you cannot continue to be sexually aroused by someone you do not find mentally stimulating, at least, not without using the emergency memory bank and extreme powers of disassociation in order to objectify the sexuality of this person.

Both men and women can engage in loveless sex by reverting to the wisdom of the British adage "Lie back and think of England." You can close your eyes, engage your imagination, numb certain senses, and have sex with anyone. We have to realise that having sex does not give us the right to conclude that we are compatible for long-term, committed relationships. We cannot go from being comfortable friends to being in love without going through the linear steps on the friendship line.

We must teach ourselves that the true level of compatibility would be the same whether we are having sex or not. Therefore, just because we have a sexual relationship with someone does not mean we love that person. It also does not mean that we can begin to censor and edit thought just so we can continue to have sex with this person. If this is the case, then acknowledge to yourself that this is a DO relationship with a functional goal in mind: sexual gratification. This relationship will not lead to pleasurable cohabitation because living together with the intention of starting a family can only be pleasurable with a BE companion.

If we never laugh together, then why are we still together?

Laughter is a cultural mechanism that has evolved from the need for members of the same species to get along.[25]

Laughter tells us that we are engaging in serotonin-secreting transactions. We learned to laugh long before we learned how to talk in order to distinguish between friend and foe. If we can be with someone for a whole day without laughing once, this person cannot be a friend, let alone a co-giggler or our least-conditional acceptor. It amazes me how couples go through hours, days, even weeks of being together without sharing any real laughter and feel that this is OK.

Telling yourself that humour is just not your partner's strong point is not good enough. One can hear Jim casually say, "Cathy isn't funny. She's just not that type." Well, let me tell you something Jimbo: Cathy is hilarious. She just does not see any point in being funny with you. Experience has taught her that, more often than not, it backfires on her. Therefore, she has decided to minimise pain by communicating with you correctly, cautiously, responsibly, and minimally rather than freely.

Cathy and Jim need to address this issue before they even contemplate having children. They need to make sure they can build a home full of love and humour and happiness in which to raise their future children. To do this, they have to find each other funny — whatever their brand of humour happens to be.

Humour facilitates the build-up of unique pleasurable moments. Such moments are deposited into our compatibility account and are the very currency we need to get us through the mundane, functional, and tougher times ahead.

How does your partner's life story sit with you?

We need to realise that if we take any two people at random, the likelihood is that they would be able to cohabit and tolerate each other's differences fairly comfortably. All they need to do is to communicate intelligently and give each other the necessary space to fill their cups elsewhere to compensate for the depletion that their toleration of incompatibility causes. However, what would happen if these two masters of toleration and respecters of each other's space not only live with each other but start to work together as well? Would this prove to be a step too far?

In today's world, raising a child is very much a joint project on which parents need to work together. Our traditional gender roles have been abolished, and therefore both parents want to be, and expect their partners to be, fully involved.

We can easily tolerate an irritating characteristic of a partner when children are not in the picture. We have the ability to belittle and ignore something irritable without taking it personally. If my partner is impatient, I may tolerate this while we do not have children. However, if I see my partner being impatient with my child, I may not find it so acceptable.

So how can we expose as many of our partners' real traits as early as possible to determine how we truly feel? Two telling sources of information are the Childhood and the Self Cups.

We need to look at our partners' Childhood and Self Cups and conclude that, even though they are different from ours, we very much understand why their cups are as they are.

We can view our life as luggage that contains our accumulated experiences. It is not necessary for two partners to have the exact same luggage, but it is important to look at your partner's luggage and say, "I completely understand why your luggage looks like that. If I lived your life, I probably would have packed in exactly the same way."

With the Childhood Cup, you need to find out about your partner's relationships with their parental figures and siblings. How do they compare with your childhood? Do you both have similar types and depths of family contact? How open are your partner's family members in expressing their aspirations, misdemeanours, and flaws? How do they compare with your family's, and how does that make you feel?

Levels of caution, openness, adventure, assertiveness and other such personality defining traits are determined during our childhood. Whether you and your partner are both assertive or not does not matter. It is a problem only if either of you sets out to change the other's character. By learning about each other's childhood familial behaviour patterns, you will better understand the reasons for your partner's nature. This may help you accept your partner's trait rather than try to change it.

Continuing with our assertiveness example, an exchange with a partner's parent can prove to be quite revealing. If I agree with my partner's mother that her daughter is not assertive enough, then I am, in effect, confirming that I, too, think my partner is not good enough. My partner does not benefit from this, and neither does our relationship.

Ideally, I would disagree with my mother-in-law and later tell my partner something along the lines of "I now see why you are sometimes not so assertive; it's because of that overbearing mother of yours. I love you as you are and completely get it now."

We also must examine the Self Cup. How ambitious is your partner? Has your partner set what, according to you, seem to be unreachable targets, or do you find these targets not challenging enough? Is there a set pattern for achieving targets? Whether the usual pattern is to give up on targets or to complete them, are you happy with your partner's pattern? Does this pattern make you admire your partner? Is your partner financially or spiritually driven? Has your partner set goals relating to self-awareness? Do you both think the journey to be self-aware is important? Do you even discuss self-awareness? Do such discussions lead to laughter and intimacy, or are they exercises of intelligence sparring in which you end up agreeing to disagree amicably? Do you avoid such self-analysis with each other but still find yourself engaging in such discussions with others?

The aim here is to find out as much as possible about your level of compatibility, and there is no better way to start than by examining the Childhood and Self Cups. Observe and analyse these cups by exercising "bubbledom"* and discuss your observations as often as possible.

How many unique references and nicknames do you have?

During the early years of a partnership, what you are looking for more than anything else is continuity of joy, a higher level of honesty, and, what is often inexplicably ignored, a bank of your shared secrets, memories, and nicknames that relate to pleasurable personal experiences you have had with your partner. These pleasurable experiences need to make you smile when you remember them. They also need to uniquely belong to you and your partner. It is not good enough to say, "Remember when we went to Naples? The food was excellent." This is a generic experience that you could have had with anyone.

The experiences that tell us we are with close friends need to go deeper. It could be the way you both decide on a game to say the word "Norman" to strangers and see how many times you can do it. Afterward, you laugh so hard that you nearly have a bodily function mishap.

---

* "Bubbledom": saying exactly what is in the thought bubbles above our heads as they form without any censorship or editing.

This experience means nothing to anyone else; in fact, it may even sound banal when you relate it to others. Because of this experience, you may start to call your partner "Normy." This nickname would always trigger a fond memory of that shared moment, which in turn would induce a little serotonin.

You need several such moments, experiences, and nicknames. The more mischievous the experience, the better a friendship you will develop. Mischief sharing is a wonderful way of testing how unconditionally accepting we are of each other. Mischief is, of course, subjective. To some, not returning a library book in time could get the blood racing and the sweat beads flowing. To others, it could be running naked through the local town centre. It really does not matter as long as it is exciting, spontaneous, and enjoyable to both. Leave without paying, indulge in a sexual fantasy, drink too much, skip a workday and act like tourists in your own town, be playful at home, sexualise the domestic chores, do something unusual.

I have no issue if, as people grow older, the frequency of mischief declines. What is a compatibility issue is if the frequency of mischief reduces with the partner but not with others.

A partner should be a partner in pleasure first and foremost. We need to have shared so many pleasurable experiences and secret codes to a point where our name calling becomes full of these unique handles.

By the time you are ready to commit long term, if the only terms of endearment you both use are as generic as "darling" or "sweetheart," then your partner is neither your darling nor your sweetheart. What you are really saying is this:

"You are the person who is playing the role of my partner in this comfortable illusion of a love relationship. It's a comfortable role; it could be worse. OK, passion and laughter are not as strong and frequent, but is it realistic to expect them to last? Maybe what we have is as good as it gets. Let's not rock the boat. So, please, accept the name of 'darling,' and maintain this comfortable illusion."

You need a much better word than "darling." How I feel about the love of my life is not "darling." It is Milk, Spongy, LM, Medea, or TWOP. These are names and acronyms that mean nothing to you, and they should not. That is the point. The names should come about naturally, effortlessly, and through pleasure. If you and your partner cannot find any such unique handles, then there is a strong possibility that your partner is not your least-conditional acceptor. You are unlikely to still be in love, and therefore it may not be a good idea to increase your commitments by, say, buying a house or having children.

Keep money out of love

If a friend of yours becomes financially dependent on you or the other way around, over time, do you think your friendship would suffer? For one thing, the relationship unquestionably begins to change from a BE to a DO because there is the inevitable introduction of a functional goal. This could invite certain thoughts that previously have not been considered.

Let us say you are the breadwinner and you want to take a more satisfying job that pays less. If your friend advises you not to take that job, would you think the advice is genuine? You must be so sure of your friendship to be able to overcome the insecurities that arise from financial dependence.

Before I offend anyone who may be thinking that I want women to earn their way during pregnancy or child nurturing, let me assure you this is not the case. What I am saying is that partners must remain financially independent of each other for a reasonable amount of time before they consider long-term commitments such as having children. Even then, they must do their best to minimise financial dependence or, at the very least, the period of financial dependence.

Having a child should not be viewed as a socially acceptable reason to give up work completely. Financial dependence damages the love and respect partners have for each other. Whenever I promote the benefits of financial independence, I invariably get asked, "What if a billionaire wants to have a financially dependent partner?" To which I answer, "Yes, that's exactly where the high family-breakdown rate problem lies: the 'growing number of billionaires' epidemic." Why do we find it necessary to use an extreme example that applies to only 0.1 per cent of the population as a counterargument to a suggestion that is so obviously intended for the 99.9 per cent?

It goes without saying that if people are fortunate enough to be able to do without working, then it is absolutely their right to choose not to. If one partner finds a lifetime of supporting another to be such an extremely negligible imposition on finances, then the capable partner should go ahead and support the other, and I wish them both all the happiness in the world.

However, this should not stop us from looking at the influence money has on love for the vast majority who do not find supporting a partner for a lifetime to be an insignificant burden on their finances. Even for those who do not need a pay cheque, the engagement of faculties in the workplace is a factor in how equal a partner we feel we are and how equal we consider our partner to be.

We must teach our children, both sons and daughters, that their main concern as teenagers and young adults is to educate themselves, develop their passions and skills, and put them to good use in the work arena in order to maximise the chances of having enriched and happy lives.

We must teach them that if they get into relationships and wish to live with their partners that they still need to work on their own personal development.

Live-in partners should take care of their own personal expenses and contribute toward the shared ones, just as they would if they were moving in with a friend. Even if one partner is a billionaire, the other partner should work on developing, or at least maintaining, a financial capability of self-sufficiency to ensure that the assessment of their relationship is based predominantly on love, happiness, and pleasure.

My advice to my daughters will be exactly that. Once they find partners whom they consider to be serious enough to entertain long-term plans, I will advise them to live with this partner but with zero financial dependence for a good period of time, say four years, and assess whether they are still in love.

By the time they want to consider children, I want them to be sure they are in BE partnerships.

Any decision to stay together or separate should not be influenced by the potential effects of survival and lifestyle functionalities such as a mortgage, clothes, hobbies, or holidays. Being able to leave a partner and hardly gain, or lose, financially is vital if we want to turn long-term relationship pleasure into reality.

If the couple gets pregnant, they can decide how to juggle their careers based on what they both honestly feel to be the best way for their partnership to continue to thrive. I strongly recommend that discussions about parental awareness take place long before getting pregnant.

Before having children, partners need to address topics such as financial juggling, nurturing duties, taking time off work, the effects on their social lives, and even what happens if they one day decide to split up.

We would do this with any business where terms on how to start, continue, as well as end the partnership are discussed at the start, not at the end when the partners have lost trust in each other and the business is failing.

I would discourage my daughters from leaving the work arena completely. Being stuck at home raising a child, getting into the school circles as the only channel to the outside world, and occupying their faculties entirely by child nurturing is a mind-numbingly dangerous path. My daughters may find themselves seriously depleting their Self Cup of love.

Having children, though a truly rewarding experience, uses a large amount of compatibility account units. Only those rich in compatibility can keep their relationships pleasurable during their child-nurturing phase.

A Thought

The number of partners choosing to remain in separate residences is growing. Such couples are called LATs (living apart together).[26] This automatically pushes the partnership toward financial independence and, in this respect, one can see the benefits of such an arrangement. Could this really be a viable option? Maybe for some it is.

Is your heart back in search mode?

Why is it that when most people see another person flirting with their partner, they respond not with pride but with passive aggression, confrontation, or jealousy?

From where do such insecurities stem? Could it be the fact that those who react in this way know deep down that their partner's heart has either reverted to being in search mode or has never really been theirs in the first place?

When the reality of our love is *not* as strong as our official committed status portrays it to be, our hearts revert to being in search mode, and there is nothing we can do about it. We can either live in denial of this fact, or we can openly and courageously admit it. Our public commitment to our partner should match our heart's true level of commitment to our partner's heart.

So how can we ask our heart whether it has reverted to being in search mode even though our official status is that we are in a committed relationship?

There are many flags and gauges we can use to determine whether our hearts are back in search mode. We can check to see how we feel in each other's company. We can ask whether the butterflies are still there, or, if sexual enjoyment is still present, we can ask whether we still feel that charge that we get when we are in the presence of someone whose mind we thoroughly respect and adore.

However, I think there is one acutely reliable indicator of our heart's commitment to our partner's heart.

Now and then, we all find ourselves without our partners and perhaps during one such occasion we meet someone with whom we make an obvious chemical, physical, and mental connection. This is an enjoyable experience that could also represent a huge ego boost to the system, but do we reveal this experience to our partners? If we hide the encounter from our partners to avoid jealousy and aggravation, then our hearts are single. If we feel resentment toward our partners because we feel they do not appreciate us as much as this new person does, then our hearts are single. If we reveal a somewhat diluted version of the encounter in case the incident was witnessed, then our hearts are single.

The only reaction we can use as proof that our hearts are happily committed to our partners' hearts is if we share the event with our partners like excited kids in a candy store. If our partners are happy and feel no threat from hearing about this encounter, then we can be even more certain that our hearts are truly with our partners' hearts and therefore we are not in search mode.

If you meet a new person with whom you click and you say:

"I'm so glad we've met. It really is a joy to talk to you. You're funny, smart, and if you don't mind me saying so, very pleasing on the eye. You really should meet my partner. I'm so sure you two will get along. What are you doing for dinner this evening?" Then you call your partner and say, "I met this person. She is lovely. I asked her to join us for dinner tonight. You'll love her," and the reply from the partner is, "Great, can't wait to meet her. See you later, Normy," and you reply, "Laters, Cruella." (Normy and Cruella are the partners' unique personal terms of endearment that make sense only to them.)

If this exchange can take place, and it is how both of you truly feel, then the signs are more than good that you have found a love worthy of being a mate — someone with whom you can confidently bring children into the world.

If you are finding such a scenario improbable, then you may not yet be with your compatible mate.

Live with, enjoy, have fun, eat, drink, travel, do whatever you wish with someone who is not a mate, but do not engage in mate-only activities. Make your commitments short term; acknowledge that you are happy to be together, but only for now. You are not sure whether your hearts have stopped searching because the above scenario does not apply to you.

So who is my ideal partner?

The analysis thus far is saying: When we meet a person, we embark on a journey on the linear friendship line. This line applies to all friendships, including those that develop into partnerships. Being a love partner is just the last stop on this line.

Cohabiting with such a person has a much higher chance of continuing, or even enhancing, the pleasure we have enjoyed thus far in the relationship. However, there is still a long way to go before we can be certain that our hearts are well and truly no longer in search mode.

For our hearts to stop searching, they need to be sure that they have found mates worthy of calling life partners. Reaching the final stop on the friendship line tells us only that we have a potential life partner. Reaching this stop opens the door to a love ladder. We start climbing this ladder with our love partner and continue to climb as long as increasing our intertwinement with our love partner keeps on increasing our pleasure.

We can measure intertwinement by examining how long we find pleasure in the company of our partner before we need a break. There is no such thing as being able to be with someone *all* the time. The question is how long does our time with someone continue to be pleasurable before we need some solitude? If we enjoy the company of others far longer than we do our partner's before we need solitude, then this partner may not be right for parenting. In today's world, parenting does not allow for much mental, as well as physical, separateness.

Remember that the key is to measure *enjoyment* of company, not *toleration*.

The Pattern of Social Change

You may be thinking that if we need to go through the six stops on the friendship line as well as climb to the top of the love ladder before we can think about having children, then very few of us will end up having children. Well, my thought bubble is saying, "Good. Having children needs much more care and attention then we currently give it." Besides, anything that could enhance the possibility of children witnessing far more loving and far less arguing needs to be given a chance.

Introducing an alternative to any of our social norms has a similar pattern historically. People notice a flaw and suggest an alternative point of view. Once sufficient awareness is raised, society begins to embrace the suggested alternative. If it becomes an alternative supported by the majority, our governing authorities incorporate it into law.

Take marital sexual consent. One hundred years ago, the idea that a husband needed his wife's permission to have sex was incomprehensible. Men could have argued that if they needed their wives' permission to have sex, then they would hardly have any sex at all.

However, the need for both husband and wife to consent to sex did become the accepted norm, and marital rape did, eventually, become a criminal offense in modern societies (Spousal rape was finally recognised as a crime in the UK in 1991, and in all US States by 1993).[27, 28]

Therefore, given enough time, any idea that aims to increase kindness and improve standards of living, especially children's, can become the acceptable norm and not a far-fetched imposition on current behaviour patterns. In the digital age, the time needed to trigger positive social change has been reduced. I hope that tolerating lovelessness in our relationships becomes as unacceptable as turning a blind eye to marital rape.

When we begin climbing this love ladder, excitement is high and the early steps may seem like a breeze, a journey full of pleasure, where its direction and speed give us momentum and hope that we will finally reach the higher levels.

If our progress comes to a stop before reaching the higher levels of pleasurable intertwinement, there is no point in pretending we are near the top. We need to acknowledge that we are beginning to find our increased levels of interactions irritating. This is the moment when our hearts jump right back into search mode.

We can try to justify that separateness is a modern, mature compromise needed to sustain a relationship. "I'd hate it if we *worked together*; we would get on each other's nerves." That may be seen as a refreshingly honest statement, but never forget that this is not possible when it comes to parenting, in particular the desire to pass our values to our children.

We will find that this is one project we cannot delegate. Such delegation does not sit well with modern men and women. We have to *work together* on this one. This is not a partner's hobby we don't understand, or a partner's friend we don't like, or a partner's job we don't think is suitable for us.

We need to acknowledge that parenting will be pleasurable in the long term with a mate-level love only where increased intertwinement continues to bring far more pleasure than we have ever dreamed possible.

I hope to see a considerable reduction in the number of incompatibles who have children. We need to be joyful at the prospect of our children adopting the majority of our partners' characteristics before we even consider the idea of becoming parents.

* * *

The aim of this chapter was to identify certain gauges we can use to determine the compatibility of a partnership. Deciding who the ideal partner is should remain a personal choice. No amendment in our thinking should ever lead to this personal choice being taken away. We need to change our relationship framework so that the awareness advice for maintaining pleasure in committed relationships becomes readily available.

We will take a look at some framework amendments in the next chapter. At the end of the book, there is a compatibility test for you and your partner to enjoy.

6

A FRAMEWORK FOR MODERN-DAY RELATIONSHIPS

It has taken me 30 years of life experience, many relationships, a marriage, two children, an affair, a near divorce, clinical depression, drugs, alcohol, therapy, recovery, research, writing a book, giving seminars, and taking part in countless debates to get to the level of awareness that I have today, and there is still much more to learn.

I do not wish everyone to go through such an exhausting journey of self-awareness, and I do not expect the young to have any concept of it.

What I wish to see instead is a society that provides avenues within relationships that will allow the acquisition of self as well as relationship awareness that will benefit our well-being, and that of our children. By knowing ourselves better, we get to know what we want from our partners and relationships.

The statistics are there for all to see that something is not right. Let us remind ourselves.

One in two marriages breaks down, and those that continue are predominantly unhappy. Broken as well as unhappy homes affect all of us negatively.

In 2011, each UK taxpayer contributed just over £800 ($1,300) (£24 billion or $40 billion in total) a year toward family-breakdown support, and this applied only to the support given to broken families with children.[29] It paid for single-parent housing support, single-parent income support, counselling, finding homes for children when neither parent could support them, and other expenses. By 2014, this figure rose to £46 billion ($75 billion), making each taxpayer's annual contribution rise to £1,541 ($2500).[30] We need to address this problem.

So how can we combat family breakdown as well as raise our self and relationship awareness?

Don't assume that all is well; check regularly

There is no better gift for a child than two parents who accept and love each other for who they truly are, two parents who express their feelings and desires and thoughts to each other as they form without any fear, two parents who genuinely get a thrill when they see the other happy. This will show the child that total acceptance and love are the essential requirements for any relationship. It is not asking for too much. In fact, these expectations should be the bare minimum.

By contrast, the worst gift to a child is a set of parents who don't unconditionally, or least conditionally, accept each other. Witnessing two people smile and relax when they are with their friends far more than when they are with each other will tell a child that it is OK to live with someone who does not love you. Such daily demonstration of friction avoidance rather than pleasure seeking is detrimental to a child's self-worth.

In this scenario, children will become confused. They want to admire and learn from their parents, and they want to believe that they, themselves, are worthy of being loved. However, if the parents are OK with being unloved, the children are likely to learn how to "manage" being unloved as adults rather than never consciously settling for being unloved.

Therefore, if two people wish to give their child the better gift, they must wait before they have that child. They must determine whether their compatibility will enable them to deal with day-to-day cohabitation with smiles on their faces most of the time or whether they will live in constant fear of irritating or disappointing each other.

Delay your decision to have children until you are certain that if your child is asked one day, "Do your parents love each other?" your child's answer will be, "Absolutely. I've never met two people who feel so lucky to have found each other. If I'm going to be in a long-term relationship, that's the kind of love I want."

Nothing more than time and regular reviews can help you gauge where you are in the relationship.

As soon as you feel that your relationship is turning from casual to committed, with the possibility of one day starting a family, your next step should be to have a compatibility-awareness session and then review your relationship once a year.

Start your own compatibility agreement

We need to learn to express how we really feel to our partners from day one. To help achieve this, the couple can have a compatibility-awareness session during which the two partners can receive some personal and relationship awareness information to help them understand more about themselves and how valuable it is to be open and honest with each other.

During the first session, the couple can start their own personal compatibility agreement. They can customise this based on what they feel to be of relevance to their lives and their relationship. A relationship coach can point out some topics that they need to discuss such as finance, socialising, solitude, parenting, and even how they wish to separate if they one day decide to do so.

This agreement would be the couple's private property, their own personal reference point that can be customised continually throughout the relationship.

This agreement should not be seen as a replacement for any religious, cultural, legal, or spiritual ceremony or other contract. This agreement is a separate entity that can coexist with any other ceremonial union.

A compatibility agreement encourages partners to promise that, for as long as they are together, they will set aside a few hours once a year to consider where they are in their relationship.

Setting aside a few hours every year to check on the health of a relationship, before having children, when they have children, and even after the children leave the home provides an invaluable opportunity for couples to see where they are in their love and pleasure. Is their relationship making life wonderful? Or is their comfortable life making their relationship tolerable?

The hope is that by discussing and revealing the very views that influence the level of pleasure derived from their relationship, the two individuals can learn far more about each other and themselves. This awareness will reduce unwanted surprises.

By reviewing their relationship annually, the partners will have an opportunity to discuss their thoughts and amend their agreement accordingly, as long as both agree. This is the very opportunity that will allow for early detection of any friction before it unnecessarily festers into something bigger.

Many relationships suffer not because the partners are wrong for each other, but because issues that might be rectified easily in the early stages lead to irrevocable breakdowns if they are ignored.

Therefore, once two people find love, then instigating their first compatibility-awareness session, customising their own compatibility agreement, and agreeing to have annual reviews will celebrate the discovery of potential long-term pleasurable love — a love both partners wish to nurture and enjoy.

This is not therapy. Therapy is what we seek when things go wrong. A compatibility agreement is something to do when we feel things are going right and we wish it to continue to do so.

The finality of marriage

Compare the ending of an affair with that of a marriage or committed partnership. Choosing to end an affair is usually the path of least resistance, functionally speaking. Both know that if their lover is unhappy, the lover can end the affair at any time with relative ease. There are rarely legal, financial, or social ties that compel a person to tolerate a loveless, unjust, or dull affair, whereas such tolerations and complacency are commonplace in marriages and committed partnerships.

Annual relationship reviews will go a long way to encourage partners in a committed relationship to be less complacent toward each other's feelings. In other words, it will tackle the very heart of the problems derived from the finality of marriage.

During these reviews, the partners will be asked:

1. Are there any relationship issues, no matter how trivial?

2. Are there any personal issues, no matter how trivial?

3. Do you wish to make amendments to any of the terms of your agreement: social, financial, parental, or otherwise, no matter how trivial?

Possibly, the finality of marriage — which applies to all committed relationships — encourages the partners to erroneously conclude that diminishing the importance of and ignoring such "trivial" matters is a sign of mature understanding. Unfortunately, these issues will fester and grow, and their accumulation can lead to mutual mistrust and a breakdown in communication.

Do not look at acknowledgements during these reviews — such as "I'm not happy with the way you seem to occasionally ignore me" or "We need to rethink how we currently share our expenses" or "I'm beginning to avoid seeing some friends because I know you don't like them" — as indicators that major issues exist. Such revelations are just as likely to lead to increasing as well as decreasing love.

Are we sure we are ready to have children?

Partners must be aware of the evolutionary blindfold. Because it could take up to three years for partners to stop viewing each other through rose-tinted glasses, the clear advice would be to defer having children until they have been together for at least four years and therefore have completed a compatibility-awareness session and three subsequent reviews. This will reduce the possibility of realising their incompatibility and unhappiness too late, when they have a child.

As with all awareness advice, people are free to make their own choices. The key difference with compatibility awareness, however, is that they will be making their decisions from informed points of view.

Pause
Purely for a tangent break, have a look at this assertion: "Apparently love can be faked for a maximum of two years, six months, and twenty-five days."[31]

How will periodic reviews change things?

We don't have sufficient data to draw conclusions about the long-term effects of using compatibility agreements and annual reviews. However, there are some individual endorsements about the benefits of having regular relationship check-ups. (Have a look at the article by Marina and Ben Fogle.[32])

For now, let us look at the possible effects using some basic psychology and, hopefully, some logic.

The lower our self-worth, the higher the toleration level would be for a relationship in which we are not loved for who we truly are.

Self-worth could be low for many reasons. It could be due to having judgemental parents with whom the child experienced a DO relationship.

When love is new, everything is wonderful and hope is high. As time goes by, the inevitable frictions of cohabitation begin to surface.

When these frictions arise, those who lack self-worth do one of three things: they either avoid acknowledging the existence of these frictions and live in denial; they try to fix things by editing and censoring their thoughts and actions in order to please and escape rejection; or they habitually resort to bickering and justify this behaviour as the nature of the beast. Eventually, all three approaches are likely to lead to lovelessness.

There is a fourth alternative. The minute these inevitable frictions begin to materialise, the couple must openly address them to find out the reason.

If awareness leads to the realisation that these frictions are results of individual behaviour patterns perhaps learned from an early age, then such frictions must be welcomed as an opportunity to try to understand and be aware of these patterns. The more the frictions are understood, the less of an obstacle they will be to the relationship — thus allowing love and pleasure to once again regain their momentum and continue to grow.

If, on the other hand, awareness leads to the realisation that these frictions are happening because of some key differences in the partners' core beliefs, then the couple may need to adjust the relationship.

It could be that one or both partners' low self-worth is sustaining an incompatible relationship and a readjustment is needed in order to avoid prolonged unkindness toward the self, the partner, and the future children. Such relationship adjustments require courage, foresight, and confidence. These traits are far more likely to be present if the person has a healthy level of self-worth.

Compatibility-awareness sessions and subsequent annual reviews will provide the much-needed self-worth awakening that will allow each of us to say, "I deserve to freely express my thoughts and wishes and core beliefs with my life partner. Moreover, my life partner must love my real self and insist that I never hide it." Without such awareness, those lacking in self-worth will find it difficult to think of, let alone proactively live by, that statement.

I believe we can all benefit from such awareness of our behaviour patterns. It is hugely empowering to know what irks us, why we repeat irritable behaviour patterns, and how we can deal with them. The sooner we become aware of these patterns and learn how to reverse them, the happier and healthier our lives will be.

Can we dare to imagine a world full of people who have become aware of their negative behaviours and have learned how to deal with them from an early age? A world where young adults learn why they resort to jealousy or resentment or repression or denial or excessive self-criticism and then begin to reverse such feelings? Think of the positive effect such a change would have not just on our own well-being, but also on our ability to be more accepting and more loving of others, of the human being. The psychological and even physical health benefits would be immense.

Each review will increase the awareness level and, therefore, a choice to continue to be together will be based on feeling loved and accepted rather than for the sake of avoiding friction or loneliness. One of the main purposes of these reviews is to make couples aware that being in a loveless relationship in today's world can prove to be far lonelier than being alone.

This does not mean that we should all leave our partners tomorrow if our relationship is not full of pleasure and ecstasy. All it means is that we must find out why we tolerate a relationship without pleasure and ecstasy. By finding out why, we could increase our self-worth and then rediscover what attracted us to our partners in the first place.

In other words, the aim of awareness and annual reviews is to take the ratio given in chapter one which stated that 83 per cent of long-term couples are unhappy, therefore only 17 per cent are happy, and reverse it.[33]

In effect, what we are doing is encouraging people from day one to bring out their true selves and see whether their partners accept and love these selves. This will enable people to either love each other's real selves or agree that they should not cohabit for the long term because it will lead to a life of friction management.

With awareness and annual reviews, such realisations are far more likely to emerge early in the relationship before long-term commitments and children enter the equation, thus reducing the all-too-common situation of incompatibles staying together because they feel trapped.

Another advantage worth considering is that, with annual reviews, disharmony has a maximum term of one year to fester.

When couples get divorced, it is often after years of communication breakdown, distrust, and lack of respect. The decision is rarely amicable, and children are far too often the victims.

Furthermore, if the terms of separation are introduced from the start and annually reviewed while trust, friendship, and love are present, couples who wish to separate will be far less inclined to resort to vindictive and damaging actions.

Financial awareness

Pre-children, both partners should take care of their own personal expenses, and mutual expenses should be shared fairly. With the help of a relationship coach, they can agree on a fair way to split their shared costs knowing that the terms will be reviewed annually.

Since the recommendation is for both partners, at least before having children, to continue to pay for their own personal expenses and proportionately contribute to the shared expenses, both partners will get the opportunity to appreciate what is involved in funding their lifestyles.

Again, no one can, nor should, decide on such lifestyle choices apart from the partners themselves. All we need to do is to make the partners aware that their relationship may suffer if one partner partly or fully contributes toward the other's personal expenses.

If one partner has to do more work in order to be able to pay for both, will this lead to a decrease of the provider's free time? Will it mean that the chosen provider may need to consider delaying retirement? Will it mean that the provider may need to consider keeping a lucrative job rather than going for a more personally rewarding but less-lucrative one?

During moments of conflict, no matter how much the chosen provider or the non-providing partner refuses to acknowledge it, resentment will rear its ugly head.

Parenting will inevitably bring about some financial adjustments. Only truly compatible, loving partners can withstand the encroachment on their reduced pleasure opportunities as a result of the increased financial and time constraints that parenting entails.

After an initial awareness session and three subsequent reviews, both partners will be in a far better place to confidently, and pleasurably, embrace the parental-induced financial changes to their lifestyles.

Parental awareness

When the partners are ready to have children — hopefully after four years and three reviews to allow time for the removal of their evolutionary blindfolds — they will be ready to receive more detailed, practical parenting advice.

- What does having children actually mean?
- How will it affect the partners' disposable income and general finances?
- How will it affect their careers?

- How will the caretaking time be split?
- How will their social lives be affected?

When they become parents, they will be entering a new era in their relationship. They will no longer be just partners; they will also be caregivers to their children.

They are about to enter into the Nurture Phase, which will last until their children no longer need them as caregivers.

When the nurture phase is over, the parents can resume their role of being solely partners.

Partners can include some initial thoughts about this new phase in their compatibility agreement from day one and then revisit it in subsequent reviews.

For example, partners can think about the following:

1. The duration of the nurture phase:
   - When will their responsibilities as caretakers end? Will their youngest child be 16 or 25?
2. Financial adjustments for the nurture phase:
   - Have both partners thought about the potential financial implications of having children?
   - Has potential loss of available income been addressed?
   - Does either partner wish to work less or not at all?

- Is it preferable to maintain existing working hours apart from the provided maternity or paternity leave?
- What about the eventual education of the child, and the type of schooling?
- What home arrangements have they made for the new arrival?
- Do they need to consider their future residential plans?
3. COF adjustments (COF is my preferred term for separations and divorce, explained later in this chapter):
   - Although no one likes to talk about separation at the start of a relationship, it is one of the healthiest exercises a couple can undertake while love, friendship, and trust are still in the picture.
   - Partners are invited to discuss what they feel would be a fair way to separate. What would they consider to be fair if they have children? The partners can then be encouraged to think of reasonable solutions for sharing their parenting and financial responsibilities and, in particular, the issue of parental access to the children.
   - Partners can be given scenarios for splitting up, such as new love or simply loss of love, and then be asked to discuss what they feel would be a fair way forward.

- This is yet another key area that, through discussion, will either further strengthen the partners' bond and trust or reveal conflicting views.
4. Social adjustments caused by the nurture phase:
   - This is the partners' opportunity to receive some awareness regarding the changes that parenting would bring to their home as well as their social lives. Parental workshops and/or literature can help.

After receiving their parental awareness, partners can ask themselves whether they are still as excited at the prospect of becoming parents or whether their new awareness has introduced some doubt. Is one partner more excited than the other? These issues cannot, and should not, be ignored because they will resurface when children are already in the picture and a change of mind becomes more complicated.

Unless the prospect of the other partner becoming the parent of their future child still fills them with pride, joy, happiness, and excitement, they need to pause. Statistics tell us that if the relationship is incompatible, the arrival of children makes it even less tolerable, and children of such a couple are likely to attract lovelessness in their adult lives.

Comfortable illusions of love are tolerable when we have external serotonin sources compensating for the adrenaline secreted while interacting with the incompatible partner. Worrying that one of your actions might upset or anger your partner is not a healthy platform for parenting. If the external sources such as good jobs, money, friends, hobbies, or health are removed, we lose the serotonin needed to combat the partnership-induced adrenaline, and the break-up of the family becomes highly probable.

A Psychological Tangent

I will use the term "mother" to mean the child's primary caregiver. Therefore, the term "mother" can apply to mother, father, adoptive parent, foster parent, or anyone else who is the child's primary caregiver.

There is no getting away from the fact that the mother-child relationship is the most significant in the first few years of the child's life. The difference between a mother in a loving partnership and a mother in a comfortable illusion of a loving partnership is immeasurable when it comes to her ability to put the child's needs first and place the child on the right track to security and self-awareness.

A mother in love with, and loved by, her partner is far less likely to project her needs, fears, and repressed feelings and desires onto her child. Such a mother has a much higher chance of accepting herself and therefore is less inclined to need the child for self-acceptance or even redemption.

A child needs his mother to be a receptor of his needs. The mother should not project her insecurities onto the child, which will result in the child catering to her needs and, in doing so, will learn to repress his own.

The child knows that his survival is very much dependent on the mother.

For example, if a child expresses a need and feels that the mother does not meet this need, then the child has no choice but to blame himself and therefore will conclude that he is unworthy of having his needs met.

The child will learn to repress his true emotions and portray a false self in the hope of a better outcome the next time he expresses a need. This, more than likely, becomes an unhealthy adulthood pattern leading to fear of true self-expression.

Once an adult, concealing the true self will be the default approach to avoiding rejection and seeking acceptance. This will increase the chances of finding incompatible love. The cycle of repression continues when this now-repressed adult becomes a parent and begins to project his needs onto his children.

This cycle has a chance of being broken if the mother is loved in her adult life. If she is loved, she can tap into her repressed feelings and eventually accept her true self.

If the mother has a loving partner who accepts her even with all her repressed issues, she will eventually become more accepting of who she is. She will begin to accept herself with all her baggage and eventually begin to unpack and re-experience being her true self in order to test her lover's reactions. If the lover continues to love the mother, she will begin to lose her fear of bringing out her true self.

If the mother does not have a compatible loving partner, her best chance of breaking her pattern and being more self-aware is therapy. Therapy will allow the mother to understand what is happening and will hopefully show her that it is OK to express her true feelings. If this leads to increased self-worth, then the mother may decide that she deserves a better relationship or owns her part of why the relationship is causing unhappiness.

A loved mother who has become more accepting of her true self has, in effect, reduced the amount of mental time spent dealing with her inner turmoil and is therefore much more likely to have the mental energy to focus on her child's needs. The mother will be a mirror for her child's needs rather than a projector of her own.

In *The Drama of Being a Child*, Alice Miller writes: "Our world would be a very different world if the majority of babies had the chance to rule over their mothers like paschas [liege, lords] and to be coddled by them, without having to concern themselves with their mothers' needs."[34]

If this idea of parenting can be recognised and implemented on a global level, I think it would have an immensely positive effect on future generations.

Loved caregivers are more likely to allow their children to learn how to express rather than suppress their needs.

Loved, expressive children will learn to be adults who are less likely to suppress their adult needs and therefore be less likely to accept lovelessness.

They will be far more likely to look for compatible love partners who will enhance their chances of becoming parents of loved children who will express rather than repress, and the cycle of lovelessness will continue to be broken.

I strongly believe that the combined effects of the compatibility-awareness sessions, the subsequent reviews, and the parental-awareness exercises will place couples in much more informed positions regarding their parental readiness and will therefore enhance the chances of providing happy, loving parents to children.

Home sharing

Many of the awareness recommendations thus far have more to do with the phase of the partnership before having children. What about those who have children and have had some awareness but now find themselves unhappy? Further still, what about unhappy parents who are new to this concept? What advice can we offer such couples?

Before I answer this question, I would like to introduce a viable option for parents who are in unhappy relationships and are therefore considering separating. Currently, we assume that such partners have to live apart and, invariably, this causes a reduction in parental access to their children.

I propose an alternative in which partners who are considering separation do not necessarily need to live apart. They can become "home sharers."

Home sharers are, in effect, two people, still on relatively amicable terms, who live in the same house and play the role of co-guardians of their children. However, these home sharers have released each other from their emotional ties. They are housemates who continue to share their children's parental duties until the end of their agreed children's nurture phase. Once the nurture phase is over, they can reassess their relationship.

When these two home sharers are asked about their relationship status, their answer will not be "single" or "in a relationship" or "separated" or "divorced." It will be "home sharer."

Please bear with me and think about this. Don't many of us already live this way but pretend that we do not?

Being a home sharer simply means the following: *My partner and I amicably work well as parents, but not as lovers. We do not want to separate and damage our children's lives in the slightest. Therefore, my partner and I have decided to continue to live together as housemates who co-parent our children until the end of their nurture phase.*

The truth is that we no longer enjoy being with each other — it has almost become a chore. In a way, pretending we still enjoy being partners is in fact causing further resentment. The reality is that we are now amicable parents and housemates.

The idea behind home sharing is this: assuming there is no abuse or danger to the children or the partners, assuming both parents still enjoy and love being parents and their children are still going through their nurture phase, and assuming there is no new love interest, why should either of the partners dilute their relationship with their children? Why not just stop pretending to be lovers and remain the loving parents whom their children need and deserve, showing their children that their love for them has in no way diminished?

We must assume, of course, that there is still a certain level of civility between the partners. If this is the case, I see no reason why parents cannot at least consider this option.

There is an obvious complication if a new love is present. Ideally, the partners should acknowledge lovelessness long before new love is found. With our periodic reviews, the window for finding and developing new love is one year. With such time limitations, the discovery of incompatibility is far more likely to precede the discovery of new love.

Let me reiterate that home sharing needs to be considered only if the partners have children and if the children are still in their nurture phase. If this is not the case, then there is no need for partners to continue to live together if they no longer wish to do so.

However, I strongly believe that our current separation and divorce procedures damage the children going through the nurture phase far more than we realise. Current divorce and separation practices make it possible for partners to use their children as pawns in their battles. This needs to stop.

Once we have made the decision to become parents, we need to do whatever we can to become the best caregivers our children can have. We need to realise that our children want and need both parents in their lives. The concept of limiting access is cruel on so many levels to the children and the parents.

We need to think of ways to maintain children's relationships with both of their parents. If anything, we need to increase interaction to reassure the children of their parents' love. Children far too often blame themselves for separations, and limiting access further exacerbates this erroneous feeling.

Becoming a parent means that, during the nurture phase, we need to make the child's mental and physical welfare our main priority. This, of course, does not mean that parents need to endure and waste their lives. The parents have the right to better lives if they are unhappy.

All I am saying is that if parents wish to separate, if the circumstances allow it, and if they can do so without emotionally damaging their children, then they should consider being home sharers as one of their options. If they feel that staying in the same house will damage the children because they cannot put themselves second to the needs of their children, then they should separate. The hope is that if couples have been having annual reviews, then they can separate using the separation (COF) terms in their compatibility agreements, which they have developed over time with care and fairness.

Therefore, if parents with children who are still in their nurture phase tell their relationship coach during a review that they wish to separate, their coach can discuss becoming home sharers as a viable option to reduce the possibility of destabilising their children's lives. It is then up to the partners to decide whether they are willing to live together but release each other from their emotional ties.

The misconception of separation and divorce

I believe we need to challenge our insistence on placing divorce and separation under the general heading of "failure." I would like to see the realisation of incompatibility, and the courageous and kind act of wishing to enhance the chances of long-term joy and happiness to all concerned, being taken out of the realm of failure and instead placed in the realm of success.

This can work if partners realise incompatibility as early as possible when kindness and logic still exist and if they celebrate honesty as the only way to maximise pleasure in life.

I would like to suggest an alternative term for separation or divorce. When one partner realises that the relationship is not working, it does not have to mean that this partner wishes to end the relationship completely. It just means that the partner wishes to openly acknowledge to the other that they have overestimated their level of pleasurable commitment.

The partners could be co-dwellers, co-parents, sexual partners, co-counsellors, co-workers, tennis partners, co-explorers, co-diners, co-concert goers, and cooperators at other events. They do not need to end all of the above if they simply no longer enjoy one, say being sexual partners. All that is needed is an adjustment of the friendship to its true level.

They need to look back and see when and where in their relationship they genuinely looked forward to being in each other's company. If they conclude that the last time they truly looked forward to being in each other's company was back when they only saw each other once a week, then they need to acknowledge that their true level of friendship is a once a week type of friendship, not one that involves sharing bills, houses and children.

Therefore instead of concluding that a change is basically an end of a relationship, we should look at it as a correction of friendship (COF).

One partner can ask the other whether they can pause and have a COF. Maybe their correct level is a lower level on the love ladder, or maybe their correct level is not even on the love ladder. Perhaps it is somewhere on the friendship line, say the "good friends" level.

This does not mean they should go back to level zero on the friendship line as strangers, or even go in a more negative direction and become enemies. There was a time not so long ago when they did get along well with each other. They may even have had great times before they entered into long-term commitments.

Early realisation of being at an incorrect level of love would make it easier to go back to the level that last brought them happiness. Going back one or two steps is much easier than going back ten steps. They need to remember that they enjoyed being at that happy level. When they were at that happy level, they joyfully existed. How is this failure? We need to realise that this is very much a success story.

Think of a boxer who is successful at a certain weight, then tries a higher weight and gets knocked out in the first round because that weight division is unsuitable for his body size and shape. That does not mean he should retire from boxing; it just means he should stop fighting in the wrong weight division. He does not need a further ten years of pain and defeat before he comes to that decision. He should immediately acknowledge that he tried punching above his own weight and then resume his career in the correct weight division.

To give ourselves as much chance as possible to make this adjustment, we need early realisation of incompatibility. If we discuss and customise and amend our compatibility agreements from day one, we immensely enhance our chances of early realisation of our true level of compatibility.

Compatibility-awareness centres

I would like to see such compatibility-awareness centres available for all of us to use as and when we wish. We should be able to go to such centres to have compatibility-awareness sessions as well as annual reviews. Let's call this type of centre "Compass."

Such centres would not create burdens on the social welfare budgets. If the aim is to reduce family breakdowns, then we already have set aside budgets for this. The United Kingdom alone has a family-breakdown budget of £46 billion ($75 billion) a year and rising.

All that would be needed is a desk in a public office. With the advent of the Internet, such sessions also could be available through remote interface. Imagine the benefits.

A Correlation

One hundred years ago, there was no need to get training to be a driver. As the number of accidents increased, it became necessary to have a rethink. Training and tests were introduced to prospective drivers so they could enjoy driving without endangering themselves or others. Accidents still happened, but at a smaller rate compared with the amount of driving.[35]

Can you imagine a world where there is no training for driving and at least 50 per cent of trips result in accidents? Do you think this would be acceptable? Would we say, "We don't need to make training compulsory, we don't need to check and see if drivers are capable of driving. If we do, we'll kill the romance of driving"?

Is it not obvious that we need some basic awareness, as well as periodic opportunities for appraisal, to avoid this "learn as you go" insanity in the name of the glory of romance? What is wrong with having a system that encourages only those who are still in love to continue to be in a relationship and to eventually have children?

Compatibility centres can offer:

- self-awareness
- parental awareness
- financial awareness
- compatibility awareness
- legal guidance
- customised compatibility agreements
- annual reviews

Can you imagine how useful such a centre could be to partnerships and individuals?

We all need better self-awareness. What better place can there be to receive this awareness than by making it part and parcel of love relationships?

If a couple say during an annual review that they are unsure about renewing their agreement, they would receive some helpful avenues to pursue such as group and private counselling or seminars on relationship advice. Such avenues already exist.

We already know the benefit of awareness in many areas of our lives. All we really need to do is to provide relationship awareness to those

considering long-term commitments, from day one when things are going well and love is high, not year ten when things are not going so well.

The advantages of early awareness and assistance for the couple as well as for the individuals are plain to see. Couples need to get advice much earlier than they currently do. Partners do not even consider counselling until communication has broken down.

Governments are forever introducing schemes to deal with this problem without tackling the real issue, namely insufficient provision of compatibility awareness at the early stage of relationships, in particular before parenthood.

Stigmatise the loveless

If we look at something as unimaginable as girls marrying at the age of nine, or as deplorable as the beating of women and children, or as unsavoury as early teenage child-bearing, reactions in modern society are shock, horror, and unequivocal disapproval.

It was not that long ago when such practices were acceptable. Even as recently as the late nineteenth century, the age of sexual consent in some American states was nine. Teenage childbearing in America peaked in the family-oriented era of the 1950s.[36]

Upon hearing that a wife was beaten so badly that her face will take weeks, if not months, to recover, no one asks, "What did she do? Did she anger her husband?" It is not socially acceptable to ask such questions publicly or privately. No matter what the woman's action, beating is never a justifiable option. Similarly, cruelty to children has become unquestionably unacceptable during the past one hundred years.

This came about because of awareness and perseverance of forward-thinking members of society who amended and improved the social-education process until a stigma was attached to such vile actions. The legal system eventually adopted such thinking.

This is what I wish, more than anything else, to see happen to the toleration of loveless relationships; the production line of soulless, bickering parents; the endorsement of comfortable illusions of love; and the subjection of children to endless displays of psychologically damaging disharmony.

I want to see loveless relationships negatively stigmatised to such a level that our legal system will take notice and reform our relationships, civil partnerships, parental responsibilities, and separation understandings.

We can start by raising awareness and hope that conversations such as the following become commonplace:

Mary: Did you hear about Alfred and Penny?
Emma: No, what?
Mary: They got married even though they're not in love — you know, least conditionally accepting love.
Emma: *gasp, tut, hand to mouth, whispering in embarrassment*
Mary: Not only that...
Emma: What? What could be worse?
Mary: They had a child!

Emma: Aaaaaaaaaaaaahhhhhhhhhhhhhh! How can they live with themselves? That is utterly deplorable. Think of all the dullness, arguing, and lack of passion that child will witness. Oh the horror! The repression that child will feel! How can people do that in this day and age?

The Compatibility Agreement

A marital lawyer once told me, "People do not realise that a marriage contract has no terms at all. It is a blank piece of paper that two people sign blindly. The only time terms are written and executed is when the couple want a divorce." A compatibility agreement constitutes terms that have been discussed from the start when love, friendship, sanity, respect, and logic are all still in the building. A compatibility agreement is not the same as a prenuptial agreement. The former offers a better start, a pleasurable middle, and, if necessary, a more amicable end. The latter is concerned only with the end.

Every year, partners can add, amend, or delete any of the terms in their agreement. The aim is to become aware of where they are in the relationship. Customising the terms is then left to the partners with guidance from their relationship coaches.

If partners wish, they can return at any time to add, amend, or delete any of the terms. This agreement need not be anything more complicated than something like the following:

COMPATIBILITY AGREEMENT

We, the undersigned, agree to continue to be in a relationship until our next review date. We confirm that we have received the following:

- Personal Awareness
- Relationship Awareness
- Financial Awareness
- Legal Awareness
- Parental Awareness
- COF Awareness

Based on the awareness training we have received, we would like to include the following terms that we consider to be relevant to our relationship (These are, of course, only examples):

1. We will alternate socialising activities between our respective friends.
2. We will dedicate one fun date night a week for just the two of us.
3. We will alternate Christmas Day celebrations between our respective extended families.
4. We will allow one day a week to each other for personal space where our whereabouts do not need to be disclosed.
5. We will take one holiday a year apart from each other with our own friends.
6. We will dedicate an hour a week to ask each other how we are feeling and will take it in turns to listen carefully.

7. We will split our shared costs at a ratio of three (partner one) to one (partner two).

8. When we become parents, we will never be critical of each other in front of our children.

9. We will both continue to work and pay for our own personal costs until we decide to have a child, then, if there is at least a 20 per cent difference in earnings, the partner with the lower earnings will reduce hours of work, but neither will stop working completely. If the difference is less than 20 per cent and neither partner wishes to reduce work hours, both will accommodate parental duties into their routines in a shared manner as well as contributing toward the cost of external care.

10. We will put our children's needs first until the youngest is 18. Therefore, if we decide to split up while our youngest is not yet 18, and if there is no physical violence or a geographical barrier, we will continue to live together as home sharers but release each other from our emotional commitments.

And so on... (partners can have as many terms as they wish)

We confirm that we are both happy with these terms and, with mutual discussion and agreement, we have once again concluded that we are each other's least conditional acceptors.

We love each other for who we are today and not for the person we once were nor for the person we wish the other to one day become.

....

Partner One   Partner Two

Today's date: ....../....../......
Next review date: ....../....../......

* * *

We need to liberate our minds from centuries of using a fear-based, possessive contract that was developed for reasons suitable at the time. Marriage predominantly was a contract for DO relationships between those who were in control (the men) and those who were not (the women).

The same reasons led us to introduce and develop employment contracts and employment law. This is the law that protects DO relationships in the workplace between those who are in control and those who are not in control.

I hope that I will gain enough support to introduce compatibility centres for us all to use. In the meantime, there is something that you can do right now to honestly evaluate and improve your relationship: use the Call-to-Action Checklist at the end of this book as a guide. You can also visit: www.compass4couples.com

We need to accept, celebrate, and adapt to the reality that love partnerships are completing their migratory steps out of the shadow of control and into the domain of pleasure, from DO to BE.

7

AND THERE YOU HAVE IT

We no longer need a partner for functional reasons. Instead, we need a friend — a companion to accept us for our flaws and allow us to feel happy to be a uniquely flawed human being. To become a friend, we need to "turn off " our brains and engage in silliness, weakness, and mischief.

I have my best friend in my daily thoughts because of all the silliness, mischief, and laughter we have shared over the years. I do not have him in my thoughts because of his sympathy or politeness. The kind and altruistic nature of our relationship is a by-product of us being human.

Of course, I will be there for him if he is ever in trouble, but I will also be there for my neighbour, my cousin, and my work colleague. I am a human being, and that is what we do. However, I will go to my friend when I want laughter, pleasure, and unconditional acceptance.

We need to realise that, today, being a love partner is just the next stop on the friendship line. Therefore, to find love, we need to find a friend — and to find that friend, we need to engage in co-giggling from day one.

When we find the person who could be "the one," that is when we need to assess our compatibility: not as a "laborious act of compromise" but in the spirit of confirming a mutual love of life and the possibility of ticking the all-important boxes of fun, joy, and mutual acceptance.

In liberal societies, most of us are now free to choose our partners, and this choice is important if we want to maintain joy and freedom in our lives.

Partners should be together, and stay together, only if time has failed to stop them from keeping each other's inner child alive.

"I loved the child in him,
So innocent and sweet,
The mischief in his eyes,
The blush upon his cheek,
The tender way he spoke,
That showed me that he cared,
The touch of his warm hand,
That gently touched my hair,
The smiles that were shared,
That filled my life with glee,
For when I was with him,
I found the child in me."

— Jean Gabor[37]

APPENDICES

COMPATIBILITY TEST

Golden Rule

EXPRESS your first thought immediately as it forms without post-editing. This is the only way to reveal your true level of compatibility.

1. Discuss each question for as long as you wish.
2. Follow the golden rule.
3. Once you finish the test, get up, hold each other, look into each other's eyes, and both say, "I adore you with all my heart. Having you as my partner is the greatest gift I have ever received. You continually prove to me that you love me for who I truly am, warts and all."
   How genuinely you say this determines your test result. The judge is inside of you.

PART ONE
1. How often do you enjoy fun things together?
2. Name two of your partner's main passions. How do you feel about them?
3. How much laughter do you share with your partner compared with others?
4. Which of your partner's traits do you not want to see in your children?
5. Which topics are easier to discuss with others rather than your partner?

6. How do you feel about your partner's level of ambition?
7. Do you find your partner's use of humour always appropriate?
8. Discuss the effect of your financial arrangement on your relationship.
9. How unconditionally accepted does your partner make you feel? Can you find some examples?
10. How do you feel about the level of pleasure you derive from your partnership (discounting children)?
11. How comfortable would you be if your partner asked to borrow your mobile phone for a week?
12. How would you rate your sex life?
13. What are your partner's sexual fantasies?
14. How often does your partner masturbate?
15. Out of all your partner's flaws, which would you say is your favourite?
16. Where do you two see yourselves in, say, ten years?

PART TWO
Remember the golden rule

1. **Out of each other's view**, prioritise the four groups below according to what you feel is your partner's genuine order of importance.

   Group A: Your partner and his/her closest birth family member.
   Group B: Your partner and his/her closest friend.

Group C: Your partner and you.

Group D: If applicable, your partner and all of his/her children.

Once you have completed the questions, reveal your answers to each other and discuss.

2. Imagine you have two children, Cosmo and Bosmo, both age 14. Below are some examples of their misbehaviour that is brought to your attention. If there was a scale that has "Punish Severely" at one end and "Completely Forgive" at the other, for each scenario, where do you think you would be on that scale? Place an X on the scale below each scenario and then discuss:

a. Cosmo gets into trouble for fighting.

Punish Severely O----------------------------O Completely Forgive

b. Bosmo is caught smoking dope.

Punish Severely O----------------------------O Completely Forgive

c. Cosmo is caught cheating on an exam.

Punish Severely O----------------------------O Completely Forgive

d. Bosmo is caught shoplifting.

Punish Severely O----------------------------O Completely Forgive

e. Cosmo is caught watching pornography.

Punish Severely O----------------------------O Completely Forgive

3. Please follow these steps:

Step 1: Name your partner's closest friend.

Step 2: Take your partner's mobile phone.

Step 3: Send a text from your partner's phone to your partner's closest friend asking, "Do you think I love *(state your name)*?"

Step 4: Wait for a reply.

It may be that one or both of you wishes not to go through with this exercise. Finding out why could hold the key to enhancing your relationship.

4. Your partner comes to you and truthfully says, "You know how much I love you. You mean the world to me. That is why I want to ask you this question: I want to try _____ with you. What would you say?"

Below are four examples of what the blank could be. Rate your level of acceptance without discussion with your partner by marking an X on each corresponding scale. Once you have finished, reveal your answers to each other and discuss:

a. Using sex toys.

No Way O--------------------------------------O Very Willing

b. Role playing.

No Way O--------------------------------------O Very Willing

c. Having sex in a public place.

No Way O-------------------------------------O Very Willing

d. Experimenting as a couple with others.

No Way O-------------------------------------O Very Willing

CALL-TO-ACTION CHECKLIST

Take the compatibility test provided in this book. If you pass, then go to point 1; otherwise, skip to point 4.

1. Celebrate the fact that you are still with your compatible love partner.
2. Make a note of anything during your test that you feel needs further thought. Set aside an hour a week to discuss these and any other thoughts that you may have. This weekly hour is your opportunity to ensure that your relationship remains healthy by revealing any thoughts and feelings you may have, whether good, bad, relevant, or trivial.
3. Set a date to retake the compatibility test one year from today.

You have completed your Call-to-Action checklist.

(If you don't pass)

4. Note the areas of concern.
5. Try to resolve these issues either by yourselves, through counselling, or by visiting a compatibility awareness centre (Compass).
6. If, within a reasonable amount of time (say a maximum of three months), you resolve these issues and pass the test, go to point 1 above; otherwise, go to point 7.

7. If you could not satisfactorily resolve your issues, then you have two options depending on your status. If you do not have children, or if your children have completed their nurture phase, then consider **Option One**. (Your children's nurture phase is completed when your youngest child reaches a certain age. It is up to you and your partner to decide what that age should be). If you have children and they are still in their nurture phase, then consider **Option Two**.

Option One: Do not further commit in your relationship. It may be time to consider correcting your friendship to a less-committed level.

Option Two: Ideally you need to become home sharers (live together as co-guardians of your children but release each other from your emotional ties). If you can amicably do this, then continue to live as home sharers until the end of your children's nurture phase and then adjust your relationship as you wish. If living as home sharers is not possible, then you need to go out of your way to keep your children's lives as unaffected as possible. This includes maximising access to both parents, maintaining the children's quality of life, and minimising any disharmony in front of the children. You are, first and foremost, caregivers during your children's nurture phase.

To find out more, please visit
www.compass4couples.com
info@compass4couples.com
Twitter: @Compass4Couples

REFERENCES

1. Lee Ray, "Divorce Statistics of the World," *Divorce News — File for Divorce?* (blog), May 15, 2012, http://free-divorce-papers-online.blogspot.co.uk/2012/05/divorce-statistics-of-world.html

2. Dana Adam Shapiro, *You Can Be Right (or You Can Be Married)* (New York: Scribner, 2013).

3. Steven Swinford, "Most children will be born out of wedlock by 2016," *The Telegraph*, July 10, 2013, http://www.telegraph.co.uk/news/politics/10172627/Most-children-will-be-born- out-of-wedlock-by-2016.html

4. Rosa Prince, "Couples to get free counselling to cut cost of broken homes," *The Telegraph*, February 7, 2011, http://www.telegraph.co.uk/women/mother-tongue/8306931/Couples-to-get-free-counselling-to-cut-cost-of-broken-homes.html

5. John Bingham, "Family breakdown 'could cost taxpayers £46bn,'" *The Telegraph*, March 4, 2014, http://www.telegraph.co.uk/women/sex/divorce/10674267/Family-breakdown-could-cost- taxpayers-46bn.html

6. Maia Szalavitz, "The Ancient Sexual Revolution that May Have Spurred Human Monogamy," *Time*, May 29, 2012, http://healthland.time.com/2012/05/29/the-ancient-sexual-revolution-that-may-have-spurred-human-monogamy/

7. "Thread — the Origin of Marriage," *islandmix*, last modified March 31, 2004, http://www.islandmix.com/backchat/f9/origin-marriage-50901

8. Erich Fromm, *The Art of Loving* (London: George Allen and Unwin, 1957).

9. Dorothy Tennov, *Love and Limerence: The Experience of Being in Love* (Lanham Maryland: Scarborough House, 1998).

10. The Mystique Theme, "Desire," *Journey to Your Soul* (blog), August 29, 2012, https://journeyintoyoursoul.wordpress.com/2011/08/29/rumi-love-poem-desire/

11. Esther Boykin, "The Rules of Unconditional Love," *Hitched*, February 10, 2013 http://www.hitchedmag.com/article.php?id=950

12. Arthur Schopenhauer, ed., "On Criticism," in *The Essential Schopenhauer* (London: Unwin Books, 1962).

13. Dorothy Tennov, *Love and Limerence: The Experience of Being in Love* (Lanham Maryland: Scarborough House, 1998).

14. Erin Prater, "Chronic Illness in Marriage," *Focus on the Family*, 2008, http://www.focusonthefamily.com/marriage/facing-crisis/chronic-illness/chronic-illness- in-marriage

15. Kathy Chu, "Many marriages today are 'til debt do us part," *USA Today*, May 8, 2006, http://usatoday30.usatoday.com/money/perfi/basics/2006-04-27-couples-cash-series_x.htm

16. "How common is divorce and what are the reasons?," *Utah State University*, last modified March 14, 2014 http://www.divorce.usu.edu/files/uploads/Lesson3.pdf

17. Meghan Laslocky, *The Little Book of Heartbreak: Love Gone Wrong Through the Ages* (New York: Plume, 2013).

18. Meghan Laslocky, "This Is Your Brain on Heartbreak," *Greater Good in Action*, February 15, 2013, http://greatergood.berkeley.edu/article/item/this_is_your_brain_on_heartbreak

19. Jon Bloch, *The Loveless Family: Getting Past Estrangement and Learning How to Love* (Santa Barbara: Praeger Publishers Inc., 2011).

20. Ibid.

21. Tara Parker-Pope, "How to Avoid Common Marriage Traps," *The Oprah Magazine*, July, 2010, http://www.oprah.com/relationships/Relationship-Red-Flags-and-the-Science-Behind-a-Good-Marriage

22. Frances Hardy, "Does your husband ever see you as truly sexy after having a baby?" *The Daily Mail*, December 15,2011, http://www.dailymail.co.uk/femail/article-2074238/Does-husband-truly-sexy-having- baby.html

23. Esther Perel, *Mating in Captivity*, (New York: HarperCollins, 2006).

24. Helen Fisher, *Why Him? Why Her>* (New York: Henry Holt and Company, 2009).

25. "Laughter, the glue of humanity?" Serendip, Last modified April 14, 2004, http://serendip.brynmawr.edu/bb/neuro/neuro04/web2/kcoveleskie.html

26. Samantha Joel, "Living Apart, Together: Why Some Couples Are Forgoing Cohabitation," *Science of Relationships*, October 23, 2013 http://www.scienceofrelationships.com/home/2013/10/23/living-apart-together-why-some-couples-are-forgoing-cohabita.html

27. Sasha Hart, "Rape, Marriage and Rights," *Open Democracy*, June 14, 2014, https://www.opendemocracy.net/5050/sasha-hart/rape-marriage-and-rights

28. Deborah C England, "History of Marital Rape Laws," *Criminal Defence Lawyer*, May 10, 2014, http://www.criminaldefenselawyer.com/resources/criminal-defense/crime-penalties/marital-rape.htm

29. Rosa Prince, "Couples to get free counselling to cut cost of broken homes," *The Telegraph*, February 7, 2011, http://www.telegraph.co.uk/women/mother-tongue/8306931/Couples-to-get-free-counselling-to-cut-cost-of-broken-homes.html

30. John Bingham, "Family breakdown 'could cost taxpayers £46bn,'" *The Telegraph*, March 4, 2014, http://www.telegraph.co.uk/women/sex/divorce/10674267/Family-breakdown-could-cost- taxpayers-46bn.html

31. "Two years, 6 months and 25 days: The length of time it takes before romance is dead," *Daily Mail*, last updated

October 29, 2008, http://www.dailymail.co.uk/femail/article-1081193/Two-years-months-25-days-The-length-time-takes-romance-dead.html

32. Marina Fogle, "Why my marriage to Ben needs and MOT," *The Telegraph*, March 28, 2015, http://www.telegraph.co.uk/goodlife/11495184/Marina-Fogle-why-my-marriage-to-Ben-needs-an-MOT.html

33. Dana Adam Shapiro, *You Can Be Right (or You Can Be Married)* (New York: Scribner, 2013).

34. Alice Miller, *The Drama of Being a Child* (London: Virago Press, 2008).

35. "History of road safety, The Highway Code and driving test," *GOV.UK*, last updated March 26, 2015, https://www.gov.uk/government/publications/history-of-road-safety-and-the-driving-test/history-of-road-safety-the-highway-code-and-the-driving-test

36. Stephanie Coontz, *The Way We Never Were: American Families and the Nostalgia Trap* (New York: Basic Books, 1993).

37. Jean Gabor, "The Child in Him," *Short-Love-Poems.com*, last accessed July12, 2015, http://www.short-love-poem.com

RECOMMENDED READING

1. Haag, Pamela. *Marriage Confidential*, New York: HarperCollins, 2011.

2. Holmes, Jeremy. *John Bowlby and Attachment Theory*, London: Routledge, 2014.

3. James, Oliver. *They F*** You Up: How to Survive Family Life*, London: Bloomsbury Publishing, 2006.

4. Miller, Alice. *Breaking Down the Wall of Silence to Join the Waiting Child*, London: Virago, 1997.

5. Miller, Alice. *The Body Never Lies: The Lingering effect of Cruel Parenting*, New York: W. W. Norton, 2006

6. Segal, Jeanne. *Feeling Loved: Finding Happiness in an Overstressed World*, Santa Monica: Helpguide.org International.

7. The Gottman Institute, http://www.gottman.com/about-gottman-method-couples-therapy

www.compass4couples.com
info@compass4couples.com
Twitter: @Compass4Couples

Lightning Source UK Ltd.
Milton Keynes UK
UKOW01f1254130117
292032UK00002B/53/P